£9.99
Bus

In this Series

Other titles in preparation

GET A JOB IN GERMANY

Your guide to employment opportunities and contacts

Christine Hall

How To Books

British Library Cataloguing in Publication Data
A catalogue record for this book is available from the British Library.

© Copyright 1995 by Christine Hall.

First published in 1995 by How To Books Ltd, Plymbridge House,
Estover Road, Plymouth PL6 7PZ, United Kingdom. Tel: Plymouth
(01752) 735251/ 695745. Fax: (01752) 695699. Telex: 45635.

Note: The material contained in this book is set out in good faith for
general guidance and no liability can be accepted for loss or expense
incurred as a result of relying in particular circumstances on statements
made in the book. The law and regulations may be complex and liable to
change, and readers should check the current position with the relevant
authorities before making personal arrangements.

Typeset by Concept Communications (Design & Print) Ltd, Crayford,
Kent.
Printed and bound by The Cromwell Press, Broughton Gifford, Melksham,
Wiltshire.

Contents

5

List of Illustrations

Preface

Western Germany has long offered an attractive option for people from other European countries, and further afield, who wanted to sample a highly-developed and hard-working culture — and be well paid for it. Now, post unification, eastern Germany also presents challenging but different opportunities.

This book will guide you through the preliminary stages of finding work in Germany, deciding what you're best qualified to do and whether you need to know the language well; it will help you to find accommodation and to settle in once you've found employment. It also discusses Austria and Switzerland.

Best thanks to Ian Foulstone of the Overseas Placing Unit, Jochen Schickert and Ingo Fischer of the Zentralstelle für Arbeitsvermittlung, Frau Grothe-Schmidt of the Chamber of Commerce IHK Karlsruhe, Andy Kevern of European Affairs, the Landdienst-Zentrale in Switzerland, Cees Sasburg of Avotek Publishers, Debbie Bushell of Solihull Au Pair & Nanny Agency, Sandra Clarke of the South Eastern Au Pair Bureau, the Austrian, Swiss and German Embassies, the Swiss and German National Tourist Offices, the staff at Tonbridge Library, the Anglo-German Club in London, Brian Harris of OCC Computer Personnel, the German and the Austrian National Statistical Offices, C Schaufelberger of Hospi-Personal, Françoise Vauclair of Schweizerische Vermittlungs-und Beratungsstelle für Personal des Gesundheitswesens, Jens Pohl of Aktion Sühnezeichen, Ursula Pohl of Christlicher Friedensdienst, Carol Rowlands of the Training, Enterprise and Education Directorate of the Department of Employment, Klaus Schiemann of *Südkurier*, Knut Dinter of the German Youth Hostel Association, Andrea Wesser of Arbeitskreis Freiwillige Soziale Dienste, the German Academic Exchange Service, all case study interviewees, David Creffield of *Overseas Job Express*, Nick and Richard Phillips, authors Rosemary Wells, Norman Toulson and Molly Perham, and everyone else for their contributions large and small.

INTERNATIONAL DIALLING CODES

The country code you dial before the area code depends not only on where you are phoning to, but also on where you are phoning from.

Therefore, all phone numbers in this book are given with the area code, but without the country code.

How to make an international phone call

1. Dial a code which indicates 'international call'. From most countries, including Austria, Germany and Switzerland, it is 00. From the UK it is 010 (00 from 1 April 1995). From Turkey it is 99, from the Netherlands 09, from France 99, from Denmark, 009, from Norway 095. There are plans to standardise the codes gradually.

2. Dial the country code. This is usually a two or three digit number.

43	Austria	30	Greece	351	Portugal
32	Belgium	353	Ireland	34	Spain
45	Denmark	39	Italy	46	Sweden
358	Finland	352	Luxembourg	41	Switzerland
33	France	31	Netherlands	44	UK
49	Germany	47	Norway	90	Turkey

The area of the former German Democratic Republic has dropped its former code 37 and is now using the 49 of the Federal Republic of Germany.

3. Dial the area code, which is always printed in brackets in this book, but drop the first 0.

4. Dial the number.

Christine Hall

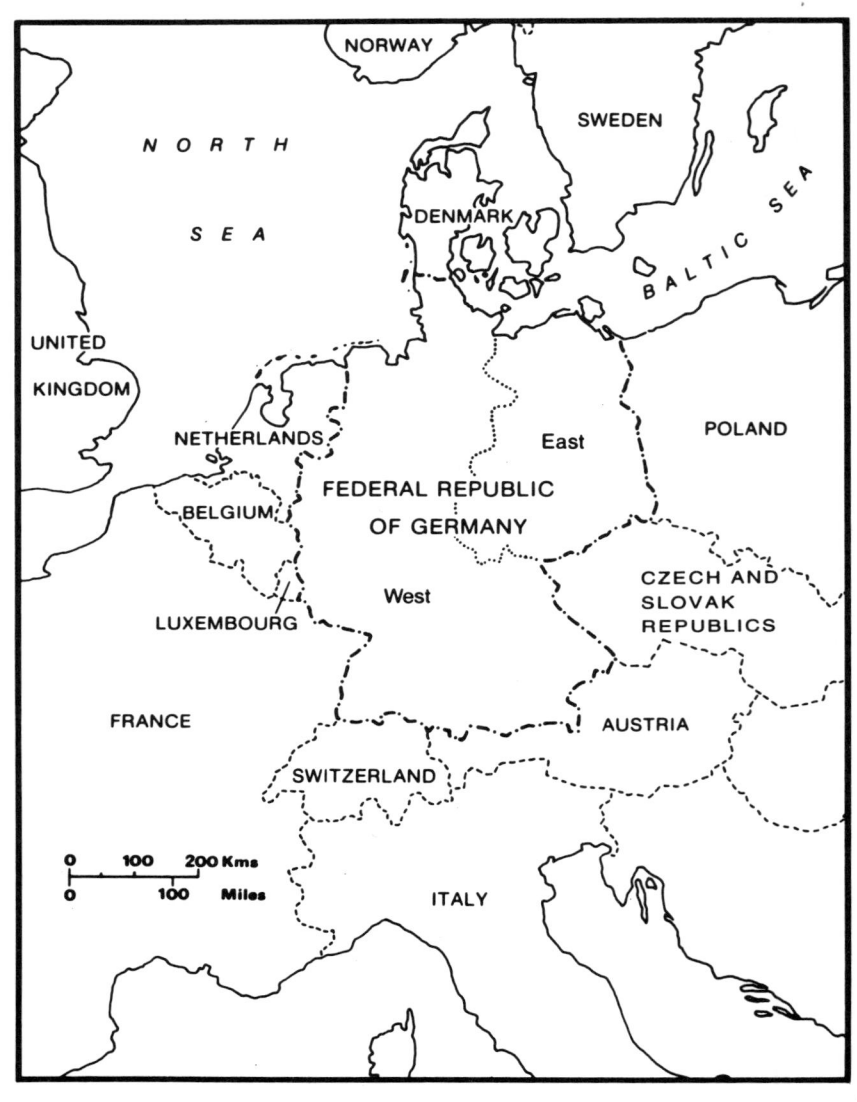

Fig. 1. Germany and its neighbours.

APPLY FROM HOME OR GO THERE?

You can apply for a job either while you are still at home, or when you are in Germany.

If you apply from home, you can keep your job and regular income until you find a job in Germany. On the other hand you will often hear about vacancies with several days' delay, and your application letters will take longer to arrive, too. It will be difficult and costly to travel to job interviews, and you will not be on the spot if a vacancy comes up at short notice.

Most job hunters start by applying from home; only if they are unsuccessful do they take the risk of leaving their job to go full time job hunting in Germany.

What to do from home

If you have made up your mind that you want to go, start now. There are many things you can do while still at home.

- Tell all your friends that you want to work in Germany. They will give you support and motivation.

- Let your German friends and business contacts know that you are interested in a job in their country. They may hear of a job which has not be advertised yet. Make sure they know what your qualifications are — send them a copy of your CV.

- Read as many books about Germany as you can. If your budget is limited, get them from the public library.

- Read books about job hunting abroad, such as *Summer Jobs Abroad, How to Get a Job in Europe, Teaching English Abroad.*

- Start learning or brush up your German.

- Scan German newspapers for job adverts.

- Consider subscribing to international job hunting publications such as *Overseas Job Express.*

- Get in touch with professional organisations in Germany. If you are a member of an organisation in your home country, they can probably give you the address of the German equivalent. The German embassy or chamber of commerce can also help.

- Register with the Overseas Placing Unit (if you live in the UK) or the Zentralstelle für Arbeitsvermittlung.

- Write your CV (or have it written) in German.

- Register with international employment agencies based in your home country.

- If you can afford to travel to interviews, register with employment agencies based in Germany.

- Consider spending your next holiday in Germany and do some job hunting while you are out there.

- Have a passport-size photo taken — and order at least two dozen copies.

- Sort out all references and certificates — professional as well as leisure interest — and take photocopies. German employers expect piles of copied certificates with each letter of application.

What to do in Germany

- Find accommodation. This can be difficult in cities. Having an address in Germany gives you a better image in the eyes of prospective employers.

- Register with the nearest branch of the Zentralstelle für Arbeitsvermittlung.

- Register with employment agencies.

- Study the newspapers for job adverts.

- Place a job advert in the local or regional newspaper.

- Phone, or write to, companies listed in the yellow pages.

SUMMARY

- Expect not only a higher salary in Germany, but also a higher cost of living.

- Most job hunters are better off in the west.

- Nurses, construction workers, engineers and hotel and catering staff are in demand.

- Make sure you are well-prepared.

- Improve your prospects by learning the language.

2
Using the State Employment Service

THE ARBEITSAMT: WHAT IT IS AND HOW TO USE IT

In the UK, and many other countries, job hunters can simply walk into an employment agency, hand over their CV, discuss their skills and register. If you are looking for work in Germany, your approach has to be different.

For a start, there are not many agencies. Until recently, the state had a monopoly on matching job applicants with vacancies. The relevant authority, which is the **Zentralstelle für Arbeitsvermittlung** (Arbeitsamt for short) is a highly efficient organisation. It has access to more vacancies than any private recruitment agency is likely ever to have. Its branches in every large or medium-sized town all over Germany are networked, so you can learn about vacancies far away.

As with many German authorities, the procedures can be a little slow and bureaucratic. Don't let this put you off.

How to register on the spot

Registering with the Arbeitsamt is the first thing you should do when you arrive in Germany. It is advisable that you have a German address before applying, even if it is a temporary one. Go to the nearest Arbeitsamt branch. Initially, you have to apply for an appointment for registration. It can take several weeks to get a first appointment, and you won't always be asked if the date and hour are convenient for you.

When the day finally comes, you may find yourself standing in a queue in the corridor leading to your consultant's office. If you are unlucky, you may have to wait for hours before you are admitted for registration and receive a pile of forms to fill in.

Several weeks may pass before you receive the address of a prospective employer to whom you can apply, or the Arbeitsamt forwards a copy of your CV to the company.

The civil servants won't discuss your skills with the company's personnel manager, or try to convince her that you are the right candidate. Why should they? Arbeitsamt branches may be understaffed, and the consultants are overworked. They are paid monthly wages, and no commission, whether they are successful or not.

If you are a national of an EU country, or if you hold a work permit, you will be treated and matched in the same way as a German applicant.

The services of the Arbeitsamt are free to both job hunter and employer. The Arbeitsamt is also the place to go if you want to enquire about, or apply for, unemployment benefit.

How to use the Arbeitsamt from abroad

You don't have to live in Germany to use the services of the Arbeitsamt. You can register while you are still at home. Be prepared to fill in many forms, if at all possible with your typewriter. Give a precise description of the job(s) you are looking for. Don't be tempted to say 'any job will do to get me started in Germany'. Your chances are better if you say 'hotel receptionist' than if you just put down 'catering or office work'.

Be prepared to wait for a long time — it may take months until you hear from the Arbeitsamt. But when you get a letter, it will be a concrete job suggestion, complete with employer's address and task description.

Write to: Zentralstelle für Arbeitsvermittlung, Postfach 17 05 45, D-60079 Frankfurt, Germany. Tel: (069) 71110.

SHORT CUT FOR UK RESIDENTS

British residents should contact the UK employment service. The Overseas Placing Unit (OPU) offers advice and guidance for people who want to go abroad. It also offers written information on looking for work overseas. There are, for example, the booklet *Working Abroad* and a publication entitled *Working in Germany*. They can be obtained from the job centres.

In addition, the OPU holds information on looking for work in specific trades and professions. Write to the OPU, giving details of the type of work you are looking for.

The Overseas Placing Unit liaises with the German Arbeitsamt, so you can save yourself complicated correspondence with the German authorities.

'Good relations exist between the Overseas Placing Unit and the

OVERSEAS
PLACING UNIT

Application for Employment Overseas: ES 13

1363/1

To be completed by Jobcentre staff before issue to the jobseeker

			Yes	No
Name of Local Office and Mnemonic	[ ]	Employed	☐	☐
Name of interviewer		Unemployed	☐	☐
		Claiming benefit	☐	☐
Telephone number	ext.	LTU	☐	☐

Sub details: M or F ☐   Source ☐☐   PWD ☐   YP ☐

OPU Vacancies	Speculative applications (see note 6)	
	EC country	
OPU order number	SOC	

Guidance notes for applicants

1   Applications will not be accepted unless the official box above has been completed by a member of Jobcentre staff.

2   You **must** hold a full UK/EC passport, a one year visitor passport is **not** sufficient.

3   All boxes relating to education, qualifications and work experience **must** be completed.

4   Enclose **copies** of qualifications and references. Work references should be on company headed paper.

5   Any applications with alterations or amendments will **not** be processed. Remember that the forms go directly to employers.

Speculative applicants must also note that:

6   Speculative applications will only be accepted for the following countries: France; Germany; Belgium; The Netherlands; Luxembourg; Italy; Eire; Greece and Denmark.

7   A separate ES13 must be completed in the language of each country concerned, plus one ES13 in English for OPU files.

8   Your application must be for work of six months or more.

9   You must be available for work at one months notice for your application to be considered.

ES13 (rev 1/93) ——————————— 1 ———————————

Fig. 4. The ES13 form for UK applicants.

25

Mr Surname	First names
Mrs Nom de famille	Prénoms
Ms Familienname	Vornamen

Permanent address
Adresse
Genaue Anschrift

Marital status/Situation de famille/Familienstand

Married/Marié/Verheiratet ☐

Single/Célibataire/Ledig ☐

Other/Autre/Anders ☐

Telephone
Téléphone
Telefon

Date of birth
Date de naissance
Geburtsdatum

Place of birth
Lieu de naissance
Geburtsort

Nationality
Nationalité
Staatsangehörigkeit

Do you hold a current 10 year UK/EC passport?
Etes-vous titulaire d'un passeport britannique/européen (CEE) non périmé et valide 10 ans?   Yes ☐
Sind sie in Besitz britischen oder EG Reisepasses mit zehnjähriger Gültigkeit?   No ☐

Driving licence	Country of issue	Type of licence
Permis de conduire	Pays d'émission	Catégorie(s)
Führerschein	Wo ausgestellt	Klasse

Town/region preferred
Ville/région preferée
Bevorzugte Gegend

Type of employment desired
Emploi recherché
Gewünschte Arbeit

When could you start work?
Date de disponibilité?
Wann können Sie anfangen zu arbeiten?

How long do you intend to work abroad?
Combien de temps désirez-vous travailler à l'étranger?
Wie lange möchten Sie im Ausland arbeiten?

— 2 —

Fig. 4. Continued.

Educational establishments and courses attended

Please attach photocopies of certificates.
Énumérez les établissements scolaires où les études ont été suivies, avec diplômes et certificats obtenus.
Besuchte Schulen, z.B: Grundschulen, Höhere Schulen, Universitäten, Hochschulen, Handelsschulen,
Ingenieurschulen, Fachschulen, Fachkurse.

School, College, University, etc *Type d'enseignement Art	from de Von	to à Bis	Major subjects Matières étudiées Hauptfächer	Result Résultats examens Note

* Précisez: primaire, secondaire ou universitaire

Professional training and experience

Give details of training and qualifications obtained. (Please attach photocopies of diplomas, certificates, etc) and
details of machines you can operate.
Formation professionelle - précisez la spécialité suivie, les machines utilisées et les diplômes obtenus (joindre
les photocopies des diplômes et certificats).
Berufsausbildung - besondere Kenntnisse, Maschinen und Werkzeuge, benutzt, Diplome (Fotokopien der
Diplome und Zeugnisse beifügen).

Vocational training Spécialité suivie Besondere Kenntnisse	from de Von	to à Bis	Machine Machines utilisées Maschinen und Werkzeuge	Result Résultats Note

Previous working experience

In date order over last five years. Give reasons for any gaps between jobs.
Enumérez dans l'ordre chronologique les emplois occupés pendant les cinq dernières années. Notez éventuel
lement les périodes d'inactivité.
Bitte in zeitliche Reihenfolge die Tätigkeiten angeben, die Sie in den letzten 5 Jahren innehatten, ggf auch die
Zeit die Sie nicht gearbeitet haben.

Employer's address and nature of business Nom et adresse de l'employeur at activité de l'entreprise Anschrift des Arbeitgebers und Art des Unternehmens	Description of your work Nature de votre travail Art der Tätigkeit	from de Von	to à Bis

---
3

Fig. 4. Continued.

27

Foreign language ability

List languages. Indicate your proficiency to read, write and speak each language.
Connaissances linguistiques. Précisez quelles langues, en indiquant, pour chaqune d'entre elles, votre niveau lu, écrit et parlé.
Sprachkenntnisse. Führen Sie Ihre Fremdsprachen auf. Bitte geben Sie an, wie gut Sie jede dieser Sprachen lesen, schreiben und sprechen können.

Medical details

You may be required to pass a medical examination before employment. Describe any disabilities or diseases which might limit your working capacity.
Un examen médical précède toujours l'engagement définitif; il est de votre intérêt de mentionner ci-après votre état de santé et les informations qui peuvent gêner votre capacité d'emploi.
Eine ärztliche Untersuchung wird vor der endgültigen Einstellung vorgenommen. Bitte geben Sie an: Gesund heitszustand, Einschränkung der Arbeitsfähigkeit durch.

Additional information

Any additional details which the applicant considers relevant to his/her application for employment including information about previous periods in the EC country concerned.
Renseignements complémentaires susceptibles de faire prendre votre demande en considération, (stages, séjour, service militaire..., dans le pays concerné).
Zusätzliche Angaben, die uns die Vermittlung erleichtern (Praktiken - Auslandsaufenthalte - Militärdienst..., im jeweiligen Land).

Documents enclosed

Please list photocopies of diplomas, certificates, etc attached
Enumérez ci-après les photocopies des diplômes, références, etc que vous joignez à la présente demande
Bitte nachstehend die Fotokopien der beigefügten Diplome, Referenzen, etc angeben

| Signature of applicant
Signature du candidat
Unterschrift des Antragstellers | | Date
Date
Datum | |

-4-

Fig. 4. Continued.

Zentralstelle für Arbeitsvermittlung in Frankfurt,' Ian Foulstone of the OPU explains.

'Information about German vacancies can be accessed in all our job centres.'

Job hunters should approach their nearest job centre and ask for a search to be made of vacancies on the NATVACS (national vacancies) databank. The Overseas Placing Unit advertises all German vacancies on NATVACS.

However, the OPU deals only with vacancies in permanent or skilled work. If you are looking for seasonal and casual vacancies for unskilled work, such as fruit picking, you should contact the Zentralstelle für Arbeitsvermittlung in Frankfurt instead.

You can also apply speculatively for any vacancies in Germany through the OPU. For this you have to complete two ES13 forms (see Fig. 4), one in English, one in German. The forms are available from local job centres or from the Overseas Placing Unit, Rockingham House, 123 West Street, Sheffield S1 4ER, UK. Tel: (0114) 2596051; fax (0114) 2596040.

The completed forms should be sent to the Overseas Placing Unit via the job centre with a CV, a covering letter, and copies of qualifications. The OPU forwards them to the Zentralstelle für Arbeitsvermittlung in Frankfurt.

'Our German colleagues them match them against suitable vacancies', says Ian Foulstone. 'Incidentally, German colleagues much prefer a typed ES13 to one that is handwritten.'

SUMMARY

● Use the services of the Arbeitsamt in Germany if you are looking for casual work.

● Apply through the Overseas Placing Unit in the UK, or the Arbeitsamt in Germany, for permanent jobs.

● Be patient.

3
Using Employment Agencies

APPLYING THROUGH RECRUITMENT AGENCIES

The German recruitment market changed in April 1994, when the Zentralstelle für Arbeitsvermittlung gave up its monopoly on matching applicants and vacancies.

In the past, recruitment agencies had been almost unknown, and they had to be licensed by the state. Such licences were only granted to agencies which dealt with unusual, highly specialised occupations — such as opera singers — or with the upper income brackets of DM80,000 and more.

'The recruitment market has become virtually liberated', comments Jochen Schickert, head of the European Placement Group at the Zentralstelle für Arbeitsvermittlung in Frankfurt. 'The monopoly has been dropped, and almost anyone can get a licence in Germany now.'

When the Common Market came into existence, the situation in Germany was slightly dubious: recruitment agencies were forbidden by the German state, but allowed by the EC!

Experts predicted that the German regulations would have to change sooner or later, and numerous agencies sprang up all over Germany. Not all of them were licensed, and it appears that the German authorities took some drastic steps.

'I have heard terrible stories of unlicensed agencies being raided and files being destroyed', says Cees Sasburg of Netherlands-based Avotek Publishers. He has studied the international situation of recruitment agencies in depth to compile the *Headhunters Guides*, directories of employment agencies.

He adds: 'Job hunters who used unlicensed agencies did not really run a risk — the worst which could happen to them was that their CVs were destroyed.'

He expects that overseas applicants will have the edge over Germans when it comes to vacancies registered with agencies. 'The Germans prefer using the familiar Arbeitsamt. The perception of employment agencies is a lousy perception in Germany. Job hunters will rarely send on spec application letters to an agency.'

You can use recruitment agencies while you are still in your home country. International recruitment agencies can be found in almost every country, usually based in the capital.

Alternatively, you can travel to Germany and register with agencies there.

Recruitment agencies — except au pair agencies — are not permitted to charge you a fee for their services.

CONSULT THE DIRECTORY

Avotek has already compiled a *Headhunters Guide* for Germany, which is a quick way of contacting employment agencies before travelling to Germany. The directory contains around 1,650 addresses of German employment agencies in alphabetical order.

'We want to supply people with the most up-to-date info', says Cees Sasburg. 'We know how frustrating it can be when you send out your CV and applications to addresses which no longer exist.'

Since the company started in 1991 it has published directories of employment agencies for several European countries.

Only 100 or 200 volumes are printed each time, to ensure that address changes can be included in the next print run.

'We make a complete revision once per year, checking on all existing addresses', explains Cees Sasburg. 'In addition, we update our directories once a month, adding new addresses all the time.' During the summer months, updates may be made less frequently: 'There are very few address changes in summer, only about three per month for the whole of Germany. This wouldn't justify a completely new issue.'

The full *Germany Headhunters Guide* costs £50. For those who aim at a particular geographical area, there are guides to the north, east, south and west, each with around 600 addresses, for £20 each. The address is: Headhunters, Avotek International, Woerdestraat 7, NL-6684 DL Ressen, Netherlands. Tel: 31 8811 65622; fax: 31 8811 61601.

Engineers may be interested in the Europe-wide *Headhunters Guide for Engineering Job Agencies*, which contains around 1,000 addresses and costs £34.

Prices include postage; outside Europe an extra £2 is charged for airmail. Credit card orders are accepted, but it is worth writing for a free info leaflet initially to find out about current sizes and prices.

The Overseas Placing Unit suggests that UK residents obtain a list of bona fide UK-based agencies which deal with work in the EU from The Federation of Recruitment and Employment Services, 36-38 Mortimer Street, London W1N 7RB, UK (a small administration fee will be charged).

Case study: the bilingual secretary

Gwen grew up in the UK and spoke fluent German. She decided to become a bilingual secretary. Within a month of finishing her secretarial course in the UK, she found her first permanent job as a bilingual secretary at a university in Germany. German friends and relatives had informed her about upcoming vacancies.

To gain more experience, and to be able to live alternately in the UK and in Germany, she then switched to temp work for agencies.

'I found it easy to get temp jobs. There are several agencies in Hannover, dealing with office and linguist staff. Many of them advertise in underground carriages and stations.

'At the moment, English mother tongue speakers with good German are in demand. I walked into an agency on Friday morning, and by Monday morning I had a job. Most temp jobs required scientific or computer-related vocabulary, translating American instruction books, for example. I did a lot of work translating for non-nuclear energy.

'Everything is much more organised in Germany. The agencies interviewed me first, then I had to pass several tests on German grammar and typing skills. You will be asked about the job you want, and your expectations. They want to know everything about you.'

Her advice for bilingual secretaries who want to go temping in Germany: 'They'll be interested in you. Just go and offer what you have. Be careful in selling yourself. Estimate the value of your service too high, rather than too low.

'For example, I was offered DM14 per hour. I said "no, I won't work for under DM16" and they replied happily: "Oh, fine, what about DM18 then?". DM18 is my usual rate. If I'm doing difficult translations, it's a bit more; if I do copy typing, it's a bit less. Someone older might earn a bit more. I am 23, and on average I am already earning more than when I started working in Germany at 18.'

SUMMARY

- If you use an employment directory, make sure it's the current edition.

- Don't undervalue your services.

4
Newspaper Advertisements

It is more customary for employers to advertise vacancies than for job hunters to place their own adverts, but both are acceptable and done.

Sometimes employers advertise in national newspapers abroad to find staff; if you live in the UK, scan *The Guardian*, *The Times*, and *The Daily Telegraph*.

WHERE TO FIND THEM

Germany has a wealth of daily newspapers, many of which are regional, covering everything from international politics to regional issues and local events.

Most daily newspapers carry job adverts in a supplement to their Saturday edition. Although many of them are available abroad, especially at newsagents in city railway stations and airports, there are two problems. Firstly, they tend to be very expensive. Secondly, to reduce the weight of the paper and transport and handling costs, the distributors or newsagents tend to take out the heavy job supplements and throw them away!

You can ask your friends in Germany to cut out job adverts which match your skills, but of course you have to be quick, so that your application doesn't arrive much later than that of a native applicant.

Papers which cover a huge geographical area — such as the *Frankfurter Allgemeine Zeitung*, which has become a national newspaper — tend to carry the best paying advertisements for highly qualified staff. Employers willing to pay DM80,000 or more per year for an employee will think an advertisement in a national paper is a worthwhile investment. It is also a matter of prestige for a company to advertise in the right papers. These may include weeklies such as *Die Zeit*.

The larger the circulation of the newspaper, the more applications will go in for each job, often several hundred per advertisement. Un-

Küchenhilfe

oder Hausfrau mit Kochkenntnissen ab 16.1.94 für Café in Lindau gesucht. Arbeitszeit nach Vereinbarung.
Tel 01111/11111

Wir bilden aus:

☐ Kfz-Mechaniker/innen
☐ Kaufmann/frau im Einzelhandel
☐ Bürokaufmann/frau

Autohaus Meyer, Tel. 00000/111111

SEKRETÄRIN
Teilzeit

bis zu 6 stunden täglich für den Leiter der Hauptabteilung Versand in unserem Werk Hamburg zum nächstmöglichen Termin gesucht.

Wir stellen uns eine berufserfahrene Sekretärin mit selbständiger Arbeitsweise und guten schreibtechnischen Fertigkeiten sowie PC-Erfahrung vor. Sicheres und verbindliches Auftreten, Flexibilität und Vertauenswürdigkeit runden unsere Erwartungen ab. Von Vorteil sind gute Englischkenntnisse und Stenokenntnisse.

Über Einzelheiten informieren wir Sie gern in einem persönlichen Gespräch. Vorab bitten wir um Zusendung Ihrer aussagefähigen Bewerbungsunterlagen an unsere Personalabteilung.

ABC GmbH & Co., Abcde-Str. 1, 00000 Abcdstadt

Diplomübersetzer/in gesucht

Zur Erweiterung unseres internationalen Handels suchen wir eine(n) Diplomübersetzer(in) für Englisch und Deutsch, Fachrichtung Technik. Berufserfahrung, wenn möglich im Ausland erworben, erwünscht. Spanischkenntnisse von Vorteil, aber nicht Bedingung. Bitte senden Sie Ihre Unterlagen zusammen mit Gehaltsvorstellung an XYZ AG, Frau Renate Müller, Postfach 000, 00000-Tupfelsdorf.

Fig. 5. Examples of 'jobs vacant' advertisements.

less you fit the description 100 per cent, replying is a waste of time.

The chances are better with newspapers which cover a specific geographical area, such as *Weserkurier, Süddeutsche Zeitung, Kölnische Rundschau, Schwäbische Zeitung, Stuttgarter Zeitung* or *Südkurier*. There are several daily papers in every Bundesland (region). So if you have a particular Bundesland in mind, or are already in Germany, this is where to look.

The trade press of the industry sector in which you wish to work can also be a good source. There are excellent trade publications, for example, for booksellers, food retailers and many others. If you live in the UK, consult the European/international volume of either *Willing's Press Guide* or *Benn's Media Directory* in your reference library. Both contain, arranged by sector and country, the addresses of trade publications.

WHAT TO WATCH OUT FOR

The name of the job is usually printed in large bold type. Find out what your occupation is called in Germany. There may be more than one term for it, as German job descriptions tend to be more specialised than in many other countries.

German law demands that both the female and the male version is printed, which results in lengthy words such as 'Landschaftsgärtner/Landschaftsgärtnerin gesucht' (landscape gardener wanted). Others put the 'in', which indicates the female version, in brackets or after a slash, or put 'm/w' (male/female) in brackets.

A salary range is sometimes given. In many cases you will be asked to include your expectations in your letter of application: 'Bitte richten Sie Ihre Bewerbung mit Gehaltsvorstellung an . . .'

Watch out for the words 'kurz' (short), 'ausführlich' (detailed), 'aussagefähig' (expressive), 'handschriftlich' (handwritten), 'vollständig' (complete). They indicate how long your CV should be (don't omit your primary education if the employer asks for a CV which is 'ausführlich', or forget the reference from your first employer 30 years ago if the documents are expected to be 'vollständig'!)

A sentence which contains the word 'Kenntnisse' or 'Fähigkeiten' usually lists the required skills. They are often divided in 'Bedingung' (must) and 'von Vorteil' (an advantage) or 'hilfreich' (helpful). Watch out for 'Sprachkenntnisse' (language skills) which are probably the ace up your sleeve.

The address at the end gives either a department (*eg* 'Personalabteilung') or a person (*eg* 'unsere Frau Müller').

PLACING YOUR OWN ADVERT

Unless you have a lot of money to spend, you will not want to advertise your services in the very big daily newspapers.

However, it is perfectly alright to advertise in local or regional newspapers. Again, you can refer to *Willing's Press Guide* and *Benn's Media Directory* for addresses in the area of your choice. You won't be able to advertise in all of them; there are too many. So decide first which area you want to target.

Don't place a box number advertisement — German employers won't bother to answer. If you want to succeed, you must give an address, if possible in Germany. Perhaps you have friends in Germany whose address you can use.

If you have qualifications and experience in a particular industry sector, consult a media directory (such as *Benn's* or *Willing's*) which contains not only addresses but information about target readership and advertising rates of trade publications. Advertising in trade publications can produce good results if you are well qualified.

Advertising prices are calculated by space (display) or by line (classified). Keep your text as short as possible to save money. Start with your occupation or qualification.

Examples

Einzelhandelskauffrau
mit 15 Jahren Berufserfahrung und perfektem Englisch sucht verantwortungsvolle Stellung, Bereich Damenmode bevorzugt. Zuschriften an . . .

EH-Kauffr. m. 15 Jr Berufserf. u. perf. Engl. sucht verantw. Stllg, Bereich Damenmode bev. Zuschr. . . .

(Retail manager with 15 years experience and perfect English seeks responsible position, ladies' fashion preferred. Reply to . . .)

Technischer Übersetzer
mit englischer Muttersprache sucht Stelle im Raum Frankfurt. Zuschriften an . . . .

Techn. Übers. m. engl. Mutterspr. s. Stelle i.R. Ffm. Zuschr. . . . .

(Technical translator with English mother tongue seeks employment in the Frankfurt area. Write to . . .)

Erfahrene Fremdsprachensekretärin (deutsch, englisch, spanisch, maltesisch) mit Erfahrung in Export, Bankwesen und Versandhandel und ausgezeichneten Referenzen, an selbständiges Arbeiten gewohnt sucht neuen Wirkungskreis, bevorzugt als Chefassistentin. Zuschriften an . . .

Erf. Fremdspr.-Sekr. (dt, engl., sp., maltesisch) m. Erf. i. Exp., Bank, Versandhandel, ausgez. Ref., selbst. Arbeiten gew., sucht neuen Wirkungskr., Chefassist. bevorz. .Zuschr. . . . . .

(Experienced linguist secretary (German, English, Spanish, Maltese) with experience in export, banking and mail order, and excellent references, used to working independently, looks for a new sphere of activity, preferably as personal assistant. Write to . . .)

Get advice

If you are in Germany, get advice from the advertising department (Anzeigenabteilung) of the local or regional newspapers. The staff there can advise you on how to abbreviate your text without losing its meaning.

Sometimes you can choose between the full circulation area, and a part of it.

Klaus Schiemann of the advertising department of *Südkurier*, a regional newspaper in the south west of Germany, explains: 'On the first and on the third Saturday of each month, we publish special pages for Stellengesuche (jobs wanted). These always draw a lot of attention.

'Instead of charging per line, as we do for the classified advertisements every Wednesday, we have two sizes and charge fixed rates for them, at a very favourable rate. Each is 30mm high, and either one column (45mm) or two columns wide.

'If you want your advertisement to appear all over our distribution area, with a circulation of just over 140,000, it costs DM45 for one column and DM90 for two columns.

'It is also possible to carry an advert only in one of the local issues, which is slightly cheaper. For example, the region Überlingen-Meßkirch-Pfullendorf with a circulation of about 26,000 would cost DM43,50 for one column and DM87 for two columns.'

To advertise, contact Klaus Schiemann or his colleagues at *Südkurier*, Anzeigenbearbeitung, Max-Stromeyer-Str. 178, D-78467 Konstanz. Tel: (07531) 999-459; fax: (07531) 999-485.

USEFUL WORDS AND PHRASES

Anzeigenabteilung	advertising department.
ausführlich	detailed.
aussagefähig	expressive.
baldmöglichst/zum nächstmöglichen Termin	as soon as possible.
Bewerbung	application.
Bewerbungsunterlagen	complete dossier with letter, CV, copies of references and certificates, photo.
Bitte richten Sie Ihre Bewerbung an	please address your application to (followed by name or department).
Chiffre	box number.
Fähigkeiten	skills.
Gehaltsvorstellung	salary expectations.
gesucht	wanted.
handschriftlich	handwritten.
Kenntnisse	knowledge, skills.
Kleinanzeige	classified advertisement.
kurz	short.
Personalabteilung	personnel department.
Qualifikation(en)	qualification(s).
Sprachkenntnisse	language skills.
Stellenangebot(e)	situations vacant advertisement(s).
Stellengesuch(e)	jobs wanted advertisement(s).
vollständig	complete.
Wegen Erweiterung . . ./ Zum Ausbau . . .	indication that business is expanding.

SUMMARY

● Regional newspapers are likely to be more fruitful than the big dailies.

● Keep an eye on the trade press.

● Don't hesitate to place your own advertisement. Ask the newspaper's advertising staff to help with the wording.

5
Writing the Application Letter

The same rules apply for writing application letters as in other countries. Use plain white A4 paper and type wherever possible. Coloured paper should be avoided, although a very faint yellowish or amber tint is alright. Using recycled paper can score plus points with many employers, but make sure it is of good quality, not the rough dark grey variety. Handwriting is acceptable for non-office staff only — and it must be neat.

For general advice on how to write letters of application, see *How to Apply for A Job* by Judith Johnstone.

GETTING THE STRUCTURE RIGHT

The word 'An' (meaning 'To') which used to stand above the address, has been dropped. Begin with the title (Herrn, Frau, or a professional title) in the first line. Note that if you talk to a man, he is 'Herr Müller'; if you write to him, he is 'Herrn Müller' as part of the address and 'Herr Müller' as part of the greeting. The titles Dr and Prof, however, are put in the second line before the name.

The second line contains the full name, the third the company name, followed by the department, *eg* Personalabteilung (personnel department). Then comes the road, the post office box (Postfach) if appropriate, an empty line, the postcode and (in the same line) the village or town.

The village or town is no longer underlined, but the extra line spacing before is essential. (However, there is no empty line in the sender's address.)

Postcodes

Because of unification, the German postcoding system has changed. Both West Germany and East Germany used to have four digit postcodes — and of course there were lots of duplications. As a temporary solution, four digit postcodes were prefixed by either W- (for West) or O- (for Ost).

Now the new system is in operation, and all places have five digit postcodes. In international correspondence, the prefix D- is added.

When taking addresses from brochures and leaflets you may find any of the three versions, depending on when the material was printed.

Examples

Herrn
Klaus Müller
Personalabteilung
Weinexport GmbH
Oberhofstr.13

D-00000 Hintertupfingen
Germany

Frau
Prof. Dr. Sabine Maier
Internationale Spedition Maier & Co KG
Schillerplatz 1
Postfach 00 00 00

D-00000 Oberkopfhausen
Germany

ADDRESSING WOMEN CORRECTLY

Until ten years ago there were these three titles: Frau (for married women), Fräulein (for unmarried women) and Herr (for men).

As in other countries, German women objected to being divided into two categories. However, there was more to it than in other countries.

Frau not only means Mrs. The literal translation is 'woman', and the gender is female.

Fräulein means Miss. But the literal translation is 'little woman', and grammatically she is not a female, but a neuter. Thus it would be grammatically correct to say 'The Fräulein opened the door. Then it walked out of the room . . .'

The women in Germany felt discriminated against by the language use which implied that they became women, and female, only by marrying.

During a period of adjustment, many companies settled for compromises. A number of health insurance firms, for example, titled their single female clients 'Fräulein' if they were under 26 and 'Frau' as soon as they reached their 26th birthday.

However, this failed to satisfy: the method seemed to imply that a woman should be married at 26, and also that she became a woman and female at the mature age of 26, whereas a male was entitled to be treated as a gentleman (the translation of 'Herr') as soon as he was 16.

Since the early '80s, all authorities and most companies have abolished the 'Fräulein', and 'Frau' has become the generally accepted female title. 'Frau' is now the equivalent of 'Ms' but used more widely.

A few unmarried females prefer being called 'Fräulein' — and will usually say so. But many ladies regard it as an insult to be titled 'Fräulein', so if in doubt, stick to 'Frau'.

Don't be sexist

The literal translation for 'Dear Sirs' is 'Sehr geehrte Herren'. This phrase was in use until the early '70s.

However, with the increasing number of women in business (in many industry sectors, and particularly in personnel departments, they form the majority), it is regarded as rude to address only men in your letter.

The correct formula, which is now used everywhere, is 'Sehr geehrte Damen und Herren' (Dear Madams and Sirs).

Ignore outdated textbooks for German which may still contain the old phrases.

If you know your correspondent's name, address him or her as 'Sehr geehrter Herr Müller' and 'Sehr geehrte Frau Prof. Dr. Maier'.

Another change which authors of textbooks have not always noticed is that 'Sehr geehrte Damen und Herren' is no longer followed by an exclamation mark, but by a comma. The first sentence of your letter, after the comma, begins with a lower case letter.

SIGNING OFF

'Hochachtungsvoll' and 'Mit vorzüglicher Hochachtung' are outdated closing phrases. They are only used if you write to a person of exceptionally high rank — say, the Bundeskanzler — or if you want to indicate that you regard your correspondent as an enemy and insult him by cynical politeness!

There is no differentiation between 'Yours sincerely' and 'Yours faithfully'. The universally used, and always correct, phrase is 'Mit freundlichen Grüssen'.

WHAT TO ENCLOSE

German employers would be astonished to receive application letters accompanied by a CV only.

They require:

● the letter of application

● a detailed CV

● a passport-sized portrait photo

● certificates of all schools you attended

● certificates of all exams you passed

● certificates of all courses you attended

● references from all previous employers

Have photos taken well in advance. If applying for a senior position they must be of good quality. You will need lots of them!

Never send out original documents. Photocopies are perfectly acceptable. Luckily, most employers no longer insist that copies must be certified by a police officer or notary.

The cost of photos, photocopying and postage quickly adds up. However, German employers will return all your material if you have not been accepted. If they wish to hold on to your documents in case a suitable vacancy comes up later, they will ask your permission.

Some of the material may, of course, get damaged during transport and will need to be replaced.

Frau   Angela Smith
Susanne Schulze   2 St. Johns Road
Kaufhaus Kunert   Oakhurst, Kent ZZ1 1ZZ
Personalabteilung   Großbritannien
Goethestr. 18

D-81369 München
Deutschland/Germany

8 Januar 1995

Sehr geehrte Frau Schulze,

ich bin gelernte Einzelhandelskauffrau mit mehreren Jahren
Berufserfahrung in der Damen-Oberbekleidungsbranche in
leitender Position.

Ich möchte in Deutschland arbeiten, weil Mann in Kürze nach
München versetzt wird. Ich spreche gut deutsch und besuche
derzeit Abendkurse.

Wenn Sie in den nächsten sechs Monaten eine Stelle frei haben,
würde ich mich sehr freuen, von Ihnen zu hören.

Mit freundlichen Grüssen

Angela Smith

Anlagen
Lebenslauf
Foto
10 Zeugniskopien

Fig. 6 (a). Sample application letter and translation.

43

Frau
Susanne Schulze
Kaufhaus Kunert
Personalabteilung
Goethestr. 18

D-81369 München
Deutschland/Germany

Angela Smith
2 St. Johns Road
Oakhurst, Kent ZZ1 1ZZ
Great Britain

January 8, 1995

Dear Ms Schulze,

I am a trained retail manager with several years' experience in leading positions in the ladies fashion retail sector.

I want to work in Germany because my husband will be transferred shortly to work in Munich. I speak German well and I am at present attending evening classes.

If a vacancy comes up within the next six months, I would be pleased to hear from you.

Yours sincerely

Angela Smith

Enclosures: CV, Photo, 10 copies of certificates and references

Fig. 6 (a). Continued.

Frau   John Miller
Renate Müller   13 London Road
XYZ AG   Little Lowerton, AA0 0AA
Postfach 000   Großbritannien

D-00000 Tupfelsdorf
Deutschland/Germany

1. Juli 1994

Sehr geehrte Frau Müller,

mit Interesse habe ich Ihre Anzeige in der *Frankfurter Allgemeinen Zeitung* vom 26. Juni gelesen.

Ich bin ein qualifizierter Übersetzer mit umfassender Berufserfahrung im technischen Bereich.

Mein Spezialgebiet ist das Übersetzen von Gebrauchsanweisungen für Computer und Schreibmaschinen.

Ich bin ein Mitglied des Institute of Linguists und besitze ein Übersetzertifikat.

Da ich zur Zeit freiberuflich arbeite, kann ich jederzeit zu einem Vorstellungsgespräch nach Deutschland kommen.

Ich freue mich darauf, von Ihnen zu hören.

Mit freundlichen Grüssen

John Miller

Anlagen
Lebenslauf
Foto
8 Zeugniskopien

Fig. 6 (b). Sample application letter and translation.

45

Frau
Renate Müller
XYZ AG
Postfach 000

D-00000 Tupfelsdorf
Deutschland/Germany

John Miller
13 London Road
Little Lowerton, AA0 0AA
UK

July 1, 1995

Dear Ms Müller,

I have read, with interest, your advertisement in *Frankfurter Allgemeine Zeitung* of June 26.

I am a qualified translator with detailed experience in technical subjects. My speciality is translating instruction manuals for computers and typewriters.

I am a member of the Institute of Linguists and I hold a translator's certificate.

I look forward to hearing from you.

John Miller

Enclosures:
CV, Photo, 8 copies of references and certificates

Fig. 6 (b). Continued.

Herrn
Dr. Ralf Konz
Intratec Konz & Co OHG
Postfach 00 00

D-00000 Wiesenheim
Deutschland/Germany

Maria Anna Azzopardi
20 Upper Garden Road
London ZZ0 0ZZ
Großbritannien

16. November 1995

Sehr geehrter Herr Konz,

ich habe Ihre Anzeige in der heutigen Ausgabe der *Süddeutschen Zeitung* gesehen und bin an der Stelle interessiert.

Ich bin eine erfahrene, qualifizierte Fremdsprachenkorrespondentin mit englischer Muttersprache und perfektem Deutsch. Zusätzlich spreche ich Maltesisch und Spanisch. Zur Zeit arbeite ich als Abteilungsleiterin der Kundenbetreuung für ein internationales Versandhaus in London.

Ich würde mich freuen, wenn Sie meine Bewerbung berücksichtigen könnten.

Mit freundlichen Grüssen

Maria Anna Azzopardi

Anlagen
Lebenslauf
Foto
14 Zeugniskopien

Fig. 6 (c). Sample application letter and translation.

47

Dr. Ralf Konz
Intratec Konz & Co OHG
Postfach 00 00

D-00000 Wiesenheim
Germany

Maria Anna Azzopardi
20 Upper Garden Road
London ZZ0 0ZZ
UK

November 16, 1995

Dear Mr Konz,

I have seen your advertisement in today's issue of *Süddeutsche Zeitung* and I am interested in the position.

I am an experienced, qualified bilingual secretary with English mother tongue and perfect German. In addition, I speak Maltese and Spanish. At present, I am working as manager of the customer liaison department of an international mail order company in London.

I would be pleased if you could consider my application.

Yours sincerely

Maria Anna Azzopardi

Enclosures: CV, Photo, 14 copies of references and certificates

Fig. 6 (c). Continued.

USEFUL WORDS AND PHRASES

Anlage(n)	enclosure(s).
Anzeige/Inserat	advertisement.
Bewerbung	application.
Bewerbungsbrief/	letter of application.
Bewerbungsschreiben	
Ich bin interessiert an	I am interested in.
Ich freue mich darauf,	I look forward to hearing from
von Ihnen zu hören	you.
Mit freundlichen Grüssen	Yours sincerely/Yours faithfully.
mit Interesse	with interest.
Sehr geehrte Damen	Dear Madams and Sirs.
und Herren	
Stelle	vacancy.
Vorstellungsgespräch	interview.
Zeugnis(se)	reference(s) certificate(s)

SUMMARY

● Type your letters on white A4 paper.

● Make sure you address them carefully, following German standards.

● Enclose your CV, photo, school and examination certificates, and references with every application letter.

● Prepare several complete application sets with copies of all relevant documents, so that you can send them out as soon as you hear about a vacancy.

6
Writing a German-Style CV

UNDERSTANDING GERMAN CVs

Thirty years ago, handwritten essay-style CVs were the norm in Germany. They were wordy creations which began with 'I was born on . . . in . . . near . . . as the third daughter of (long list of titles and achievements, followed by name) . . . and his wife . . .' and mentioned every subsequent move the family made to another village or address.

Some German textbooks, even for business German, still give examples of such CVs — beware of them!

Today, employers prefer a concise, typewritten, tabular (tabellarisch) CV (Lebenslauf). Very few employers like handwritten CVs, and they will always say so in their job adverts.

The main difference between a British and a German CV is that the German one is always arranged in chronological order, listing first your **education** (from primary school to university), then your **employment** history (from your first job to your current occupation). In the UK, employers prefer to read about recent employment before they dig into your past.

Differences to watch out for include figures. The Germans use a comma where the British use a full stop, and a full stop where the British use a comma. For example, 1,000,000 becomes 1.000.000, and 1.5 becomes 1,5.

The figures for seven and one differ from the British figures. Take care when a handwritten CV is required, and also when handwriting addresses, or your letters will be delivered to the wrong house. For one, write ⅂, not 1. For seven, write ⁊, not 7.

MAKING THE MOST OF YOUR HOBBIES

When listing your hobbies, try and include one **intellectual** interest (reading, writing poetry, learning languages), one **creative** (painting, photography, pottery) and one type of **sport**.

German personnel managers want to see if you are a 'well-rounded' personality. The creative hobby is essential if you apply for a management job, as it can help to balance stress.

Sports are even more important. In certain industries, especially in banking and finance, and high powered management positions, your CV may end up on the rejects pile without further consideration if you don't mention sports. Sport is essential for your health, German personnel managers argue.

It does not matter which type of sport you prefer. You can do anything from folk dancing to long distance running. However, you gain extra plus points if you mention **team sports** (football, volleyball etc). Risky sports (alpine skiing, motor racing, rugby) should be avoided, or your employer fears that you will be in hospital with broken ribs for several weeks every year.

WHAT TO TRANSLATE

If you are doing a DIY translation of your CV, the question arises what to translate and what to leave in your native language.

Addresses — your own or your employer's — should never be translated. Otherwise the reply will never arrive at the right address.

Your telephone number is another matter. There are many different ways of indicating international dialling codes, but they are different from country to country. So if you want to send your CV to German, Swiss and Austrian employers, it is best to just use the area code and phone number only, without the country code.

It is more difficult with job titles and qualifications. On the one hand, there is rarely a precise equivalent in German. On the other hand, your prospective employer may not understand your experience and skills if they are described in a foreign language.

The best idea is to give job titles and qualifications in your native language, but add a brief translation in brackets.

Skills are measured in different ways. For example, in Germany shorthand speed is calculated in syllables per minute, not in words per minute. Typing skills are measured in letters per minute, not in words, because German words can be anything between two and fifty letters long!

If you know your typing speed in words per minute, multiply it by five, and you get your approximate typing speed in letters per minute.

USING A CV BUREAU

If you are uncertain about presentation, translation, grammar, spelling and style, you should consider using a CV bureau. This is advisable if you are already in Germany. Take either your CV in your mother tongue or your draft German CV to the bureau as a basis for discussion and work.

It is more difficult if you are still in your home country. CV writers who are not only fluent in German, but up to date with developments in language and style, are rare.

USEFUL WORDS AND PHRASES

Abendkurs/Abendschule	evening classes.
Adresse	address.
Arbeitgeber	employer.
Berufsausbildung/Lehre	training, apprenticeship.
Berufserfahrung	professional/work experience.
Familienstand	marital status.
fließend	fluent.
Geburtsdatum	date of birth.
Geburtsort	place of birth.
geschieden	divorced.
getrennt lebend	separated.
Grundschule	primary school.
Hobbys	hobbies.
Kurzschrift/Stenografie	shorthand.
Lebenslauf	CV.
Maschinenschreiben	typing.
Nachname	surname.
Name	name.
Postleitzahl	post code.
Referenzen	references.
Schulbildung	school and college education.
Sprachkenntnisse	knowledge of languages.
Staatsangehörigkeit	nationality.
Studium	university studies.
Telefon, Telefonnummer	telephone.
Textverarbeitung	wordprocessing.
unverheiratet/ledig	single.
verheiratet	married.
verwitwet	widowed.

Lebenslauf

Name:	Angela Smith
Adresse:	2 St. John's Road Oakhurst, Kent ZZ1 1ZZ Großbritannien Telefon (00000) 000 000
Geburtsdatum:	15. Januar 1962
Geburtsort:	Oakhurst
Staatsangehörigkeit:	Britisch
Familienstand:	geschieden
Schulbildung:	1968-1974 Oakhurst Primary School 1974-1979 Oakhurst Secondary School
Berufserfahrung:	1979-1980 Trainee retail manager (Auszubildende Einzelhandelskauffrau) Desirée Fashion Boutique, Oakhurst 1980-1985 Assistant manager (Stellvertretende Managerin) Desirée Fashion Boutique, Oakhurst Seit 1985 Deputy Managing Director (Stellvertretende Geschäftsführerin) Rhona's Fashions, London
Hobbys:	Lesen, reiten, fotografieren
Sprachkenntnisse:	Englisch (Muttersprache) Deutsch (3 Jahre Abendkurs)
Weitere Informationen:	Führerschein

Fig. 7 (a). Sample German-style CV.

Lebenslauf

Name:	John Miller
Adresse:	13 London Road
	Little Lowerton, AA0 AA
	Großbritannien
	Telefon (00000) 000 000
Geburtsdatum:	1. Juli 1964
Geburtsort:	Little Lowerton
Staatsangehörigkeit:	Britisch
Familienstand:	ledig
Schulbildung:	1969-1975 Lowerton Primary School
	1975-1982 Lowerton Secondary School
	A-levels (entspricht dem Abitur) in
	Mathematik, Englisch, Deutsch und
	Wirtschaftskunde
Berufsausbildung:	Januar 1985 einmonatiger TEFL-Kurs
	für Englischlehrer, Lowerton Language
	Centre
Berufserfahrung:	1982-1983 Au Pair in Deutschland
	Familie Müller, Mühlingen
	1984 — ein Jahr Reise um die Welt mit
	Gelegenheitsarbeiten
	1985-1987 Englischlehrer mit Volun-
	tary Service Overseas
	(entspricht dem Deutschen Entwick-
	lungshilfedienst) an einem Gymnasium
	in Tansania
	1987-1991 Technischer Übersetzer
	(Spezialgebiet Gebrauchsanweisungen
	für Schreibmaschinen und Computer)
	Computech Warner, London
	1991-1993 Englischlehrer an einer staat-
	lichen Grund- und Mittelschule in Prag
	Seit 1993: freiberuflicher Übersetzer
Hobbys:	Reisen, Karate, Töpfern
Sprachkenntnisse:	Englisch (Muttersprache)
	Deutsch (fließend in Wort und Schrift)

Fig. 7 (b). Sample German-style CV.

Lebenslauf

Name:	Maria Anna Azzopardi
Adresse:	20 Upper Garden Road
	London ZZ0 0ZZ
	Großbritannien
	Telefon (00000) 000 000
Geburtsdatum:	12. February 1954
Geburtsort:	Valetta, Malta
Staatsangehörigkeit:	Britisch
Familienstand:	ledig
Schulbildung:	1959-1963 Grundschule in Valetta, Malta
	1963-1973 St Ruth's Boarding School For Girls, London (Internat)
	1973-1976 Uppertown Business College (Wirtschaftsschule). Abschluss als Fremdsprachensekretärin.
Berufserfahrung:	1977-1980 Sekretärin in der Exportabteilung, Intertrade Uppertown.
	1980-1985 Fremdsprachen-korrespondentin, XYZ Bank, London
	Seit 1985: Abteilungsleiterin Kundenbetreuung, Smith & Co, London
Schreibtechnische Fahigkeiten:	Deutsche, englische und spanische Stenografie (100 Silben pro Minute)
	Maschinenschreiben (300 Anschläge pro Minute)
	Textverarbeitung (WordPerfect, Microsoft Word, Wordstar, IBM Displaywrite)
	Desktop Publishing (Pagemaker)
Sprachkenntnisse:	Englisch (Muttersprache)
	Maltesisch (Muttersprache)
	Deutsch (fließend)
	Spanisch (fließend)
	Französisch (Grundkenntnisse)

Fig. 7 (c). Sample German-style CV.

55

Vorname(n)	first/Christian name(s).
Vorwahl	area code.
Weitere Informationen	additional information.
Weiterführende Schule(n)	secondary school(s).
Wohnort	town, village of residence.

SUMMARY

● Arrange your CV in chronological order starting with your education and finishing with your current employment.

● Choose your hobbies carefully; remember what they will reveal about your personality.

● Give a translation of your job title and qualifications.

● Don't translate your address.

● Consider using a CV bureau or a qualified translator to make sure the grammar, spelling and phrases in your CV are correct.

● Unless the employer asks for a handwritten resumé, send a typewritten CV in tabular form.

7
Preparing Yourself
for the Interview

GETTING READY FOR THE INTERVIEW

There are good books available to help you prepare for a job interview, such as *How to Pass that Interview* by Judith Johnstone. As many principles for interviewing apply all over the world, it is a good idea to prepare for your interview in the same way you would for one in your home country.

But certain things differ from country to country. Unfortunately, there are no books which prepare specifically for a job interview abroad.

COPING WITH THE DIFFERENCES

Interviews in Germany tend to be slightly more formal than in the UK. Find out well in advance if the interview is going to be conducted in your mother tongue or in German. If you have to struggle through a German language interview, make sure you can answer the most likely questions fluently, and can explain your professional background in German.

Remember the German obsession with **references** and **certificates**. Take all the originals with you. Most employers won't bother, but some insist on examining the originals and comparing them with the photocopies you have sent.

Be punctual
The average employer places a lot of emphasis on **punctuality**. Make sure you arrive well in advance, even if waiting in the reception room increases your nervousness. It can be a good idea to arrive in Germany the evening before, in case of public transport breakdowns or strikes (although neither is likely in Germany).

Remember that if your employer suggests you come along at

'halb zehn', the literal translation is 'half ten', but what she means is 'half nine'.

The Germans measure the time this way. After all, the tenth hour is not full yet, the clock is only on its way there, so it's half ten, isn't it?

Examples

- 9.00 = neun, translates: nine, means: nine

- 9.15 = viertel zehn, translates: quarter ten, means: quarter past nine

- 9.30 = halb zehn, translates: half ten, means: half nine

- 9.45 = dreiviertel zehn, translates: three quarters ten, means: quarter to ten.

Confusing? If in doubt, double check with the prospective employer or her secretary: 'You mean 9.30 or 10.30?', but don't just turn up an hour late.

If you book your flight at least two weeks in advance, arrange your interview for either Friday or Monday, and spend the weekend in Germany you may obtain favourable air rates. It can work out cheaper to spend a weekend (including accommodation) in Germany than to book a return flight for the same day.

How to dress

Germans dress slightly less formally for job interviews than the British. For example, a candidate for the job of a secretary will look overdressed in a smart suit, unless she is a high level PA. A plain dark skirt and a white or cream long-sleeved blouse are more appropriate.

QUESTIONS YOU WILL BE ASKED

Why do you want to go abroad?

You can be sure that this question will come up. Surprisingly, it is the question at which most candidates fail. Many have not thought enough about their motivation to be able to give a proper reply!

The most frequent answer is 'Well, I have always wanted to work abroad'. But this is the wrong answer. It shows that you don't know what you want, that you have no plans and goals.

Look up the answers about your motivation in Chapter 1, and select the ones which are likely to please your employer. Of course, you can edit them.

There are three groups of reasons for going abroad: personal, professional and caring.

You should state at least **two reasons**, one professional and one personal.

Among the personal reasons it would be foolish to admit that you 'want to get away from it all' or that you are 'disillusioned with life in . . .'. Your employer might interpret it as 'has failed in his/her life so far'. If you want to mention this reason at all, dress it up in the phrase' I am ready for a change'.

'I want adventure' is not the wisest choice either, unless you are applying for the position of expedition leader! 'I am looking for a challenge', however, is fine. Be careful with admissions that you are looking for power and prestige.

Personal reasons for which you get a lot of ticks against your name are the ones which indicate that you want to learn something, such as 'I want to widen my horizon', or 'for personal growth'.

Good professional reasons are 'I want to further my career' or 'it fits in with my long term career plans' (be prepared to explain how). 'To learn how things are done in another country' and 'to acquire new skills' are also very good.

'To escape (the threat of) unemployment' is an acceptable reason, as long as you can back it up with others.

Caring reasons are acceptable for every type of job, and necessary for social and voluntary work.

The problem is how to express them. Some phrases — such as 'I want to do good' — sound silly, others sound patronising. 'To share my skills' is often the most appropriate phrase. Alternatively, say 'I have had the privilege of a good education, and I want to help others to have the same'.

Even if you are applying to a church organisation, be careful how you present the reason that you want to 'convert people', 'help them find the true belief' etc, unless you want to be a priest or missionary.

Why do you want to work in Germany?

Again, most candidates will say 'I have always wanted to work abroad, and Germany has the best working conditions and I don't need a work permit'. This reply may be honest, but it is wrong. It shows that you have no deep interest in the German country.

Perhaps you really don't mind where you work, as long as it is in a foreign country. But you must not admit it.

Say something flattering about Germany. Perhaps you have German friends who are such lovely people. You may praise the German mentality (which you know from last year's holiday in the Black Forest) or the technical standards and precision (which you know from doing business with Germany). The particular industry sector has an excellent reputation in the world. Praise the German cuisine with its Knödel and Sauerkraut if you cannot think of anything else, but praise something!

Why do you want to leave your country?

This question is a trap. State categorically (whether it is true or not) that you are not trying to get away from something. You want to move towards something. You are an active, not a reactive person.

What problems do you expect to have?

This is another unavoidable question. Be careful. If you reply 'none', you have lost the game. This answer shows that you haven't thought things through yet.

The best strategy is to mention **two potential difficulties** — and present these together with **solutions**.

Most applicants for jobs abroad are concerned about loneliness, adapting and health. You can admit to any of them. For example: 'The first few weeks may be a period of isolation. I will learn German as quickly as possible, and join a club or hobby group on my arrival.' — 'Perhaps there are some German customs which seem a bit strange at first. I will ask colleagues for advice on how to respond.'

What will you do if . . .?

Often, the employer will mention additional problem situations and how you will cope with them: homesickness, leaving friends and family behind, even celibacy. The best strategy is to admit that these situations can be difficult, but that you can solve the problems easily. However, you can only be convincing if you have thought carefully about potential problems and their solutions before going to the interview.

Are you sure you can do the job?

No modest 'I will do my best' here! A confident 'Ja' is required.

How much do you expect to earn?

A tricky question, particularly if you have no idea what the wages levels are like. But you must come up with an answer. If you state a 'between . . . and' range, you will be offered the bottom sum, even if the employer had been willing to pay more. If in doubt, ask for more than you expect.

You can always negotiate downwards, and German employers are more likely to be impressed if a candidate rates his or her own services highly.

If you want to be vague, you can use either of the following: 'My present salary is . . ., and naturally I would expect to improve my situation with the move.' Or: 'My present salary is . . ., but I am prepared to take a drop initially for the right job.' But you must be clear in your mind whether you want to earn more or are prepared to take less than you get at present.

SUMMARY

- Anticipate the likely questions and prepare fluent answers.

- Be punctual — and be sure of the time of your appointment.

- Think carefully about your reasons for applying for the job and decide which of them are likely to impress the interviewer.

- Dress neatly, but not too formally.

- Be clear in your mind about the salary you are expecting.

- During the interview, show a positive attitude towards Germany.

8
Training for a New Career

Trainees are wanted in Germany. Training places outnumber apprenticeship applicants in both the former GDR and the former FRG. In September 1992 there were 123,500 training vacancies — and just 11,800 applicants!

At first glance, these figures appear low. But most Germans take up a training position after leaving school in summer, so the September statistics cover only unsuccessful jobhunters and unfilled vacancies.

For young men, the most popular training scheme in Germany is Kraftfahrzeugmechaniker (**car mechanic**), followed by Elektroinstallateur (**electrician**) and Maurer (**bricklayer**).

Among women, Bürokauffrau (**office manager**) is the number one, followed by Kauffrau im Einzelhandel (**retail manager**) and Arzthelferin (**surgery assistant**).

Although there are 376 different apprenticeships available, almost a quarter of male and a third of female trainees are concentrated in five types of training.

WHAT TO EXPECT

The German training system is thorough and strictly regulated by the chambers of industry, trade and commerce. Almost every trade — from ladies' fashion tailor to banker, from car mechanic to retail manager — requires a two to three year training period, during which the trainee will work in all departments and sectors of the industry.

Two mornings per week at college are advisable (obligatory if you are under 18) as the training schemes are based on this dual education system. College hours are counted as work hours. Trainees study some general subjects — usually German essay writing and some basic politics — as well as theoretical subjects connected with their career — *eg* literature for booksellers, accounting for foreign trade managers.

These theoretical subjects form part of the final examination which leads to the Chamber of Commerce or Chamber of Trade Diploma (Kaufmannsgehilfenbrief or Gesellenbrief).

There are regional differences in the availability of jobs: in western Berlin, for instance, the number of vacancies almost equals the number of applicants. In southern Bavaria, each aspiring trainee can choose among three jobs.

Where places are easiest to find

Even in the eastern part of Germany, there are more vacancies than applicants. Only around the Polish and Czech borders is it difficult to find an apprenticeship.

The **building**, **catering** and **retail** sectors in particular are looking for trainees. In eastern Germany, however, the retail and service industries cannot provide enough jobs for all the applicants.

Administration, **trade**, **computing** and **managerial** traineeships are popular with young Germans and can be difficult to obtain for foreigners.

If you are keen to have a career which involves these skills, your best bet is to train for Einzelhandelskaufmann/Einzelhandelskauffrau (**retail manager**). Initial wages are low, and work hours inconvenient (no Sunday trading, though). But once you've got your Kaufmannsgehilfenbrief (Chamber of Commerce diploma) in your pocket, your job and career prospects are excellent.

Major retail chains are constantly looking for qualified, ambitious retail staff who are able and willing to take on more responsibility. With discipline, ambition, hard work and fluent German, you are likely to climb the ladder rapidly. Some big chains offer special training schemes for graduates which last one year instead of three.

You can contact the personnel department (Personalabteilung) of major retail chains directly to apply for a trainee job. Allkauf, Hertie, Kaufhof, Woolworth, Aldi, Edeka, Rewe, Spar and Kaufhalle are among the largest. The German Embassy is able to supply addresses if you send a stamped addressed envelope.

Hairdressing is another promising career for foreign nationals. Again, the initial pay is low (by German standards!), but job prospects are good, particularly in the western part of Germany. You don't even have to speak fluent German initially, but you need to pick up the terminology of the trade and some small-talk phrases quickly.

The share of foreign trainees is increasing — from 57,000 in

1986 to 98,000 in 1990, and foreign nationals account for seven per cent of all trainees.

How much will you earn?

Trainee wages are paid monthly and are not very high — just enough for survival in a tiny bedsit on basic food. In the second and third year the apprentice earns a bit more than in the first year. There are huge differences between the various sectors, however.

Trainee tailors and photographers are at the bottom end of the wage list; administration and office management trainees get a bit more. Technical jobs are generally better paid than office work, and apprentices in the building or mining sector can afford a comfortable bedsit!

You won't be the only grown-up among youngsters: many Germans go to school until they are 20 or 21 to obtain the higher school leaving certificate (Abitur), often followed by six to eight years at university, before they sign up for a training contract.

How to apply

Most employers inform the local Arbeitsamt about training vacancies. If you are looking for a training placement, you can register free of charge with the Arbeitsamt, either by going to the nearest local branch or by writing to Overseas Placing Unit (if you are living in the UK) or to the Zentralstelle für Arbeitsvermittlung (if you are living in another country).

After a few weeks, you will receive one or more cards with the address of an employer and the type of training they offer. You send your letter of application, CV, photo, certificates and references directly to the suggested employer. The Arbeitsamt will keep you on the books until you are matched.

The Arbeitsamt is very efficient when it comes to finding training placements.

Alternatively, you can write to companies in the relevant industry sector, study newspaper advertisements or place an advertisement yourself.

Most employers take trainees from January or from September.

HOW TO COMPARE QUALIFICATIONS

How can job seekers have the same chances when looking for work in other European countries, if employers are not sure what their qualifications are? Every country has its own system of training and its own idea of which job needs what qualification.

To make life easier for employers, job hunters, and national authorities, the European Commission and the European Centre for the Development of Vocational Training have got together to work on the comparability of vocational training qualifications. Not easy!

Some occupations are the same everywhere. Others may be defined more specifically. If the industry in which you want to train is larger and stronger in Germany than in your home country, there are likely to be several different training schemes and qualifications instead of just one, giving you a more specialised training.

Examples

An aircraft mechanic is not an aircraft mechanic, and an upholsterer is not an upholsterer everywhere. In the UK you can train for 'aircraft mechanic'. In Germany, you have to decide between Fluggerätmechaniker (aircraft mechanic), Flugtriebwerkmechaniker (aircraft propulsion system mechanic) and Fluggerätbauer (aircraft maker).

In the UK there is the occupation upholsterer. In Germany there is not only the Polsterer, but also the Fahrzeugpolsterer (motor vehicle upholsterer), the Sattler (heavy leather goods maker), and the Raumausstatter (interior decorator).

They all fulfil the following description from the *Comparability Information Sheet for an Upholsterer* (an official publication of the European Communities): 'A skilled worker capable of producing in an autonomous and competent manner upholstery and upholstered cushions for different types of furniture, vehicles and other uses and of repairing the same'.

According to the information sheet, tasks include: 'Selecting and preparing the materials, auxiliary materials and tools. Measuring and calculating surfaces. Constructing various spring systems. Making upholstery, *eg* from boards, mats and moulded parts. Performing shaping and fabric matching work. Cutting material such as leather, synthetic and other materials. Covering upholstery. Making and attaching ornamentation such as frills, trimmings, buttons. Carrying out intermediate and final checks. Servicing and maintaining machines, tools and equipment. Recording technical data and work results.'

It can be imagined how helpful these Europe-wide job descriptions are for employers who want to know how much a foreign qualification is worth, particularly as the information sheet describes the differences as well!

They are also invaluable if you are describing your own qualifications in your CV, as the dictionary is not always a great help in these matters.

Not all occupations have been covered yet, but information sheets are available for a variety of jobs, from auto paint sprayer to goat herdsman, from wine waiter/waitress to telecommunications fitter, from retail travel agency clerk to dockyard crane driver. It is worth asking if your skills area has been covered yet.

If you are an EU national holding qualifications in any of the occupations already covered by *Comparability*, or if you plan to train for one of these occupations, you can obtain copies of the appropriate information sheets from the comparability co-ordinator at the Employment Department.

CONTACT ADDRESSES

German Chamber of Commerce
Deutsche Industrie- und Handelskammer, 16 Buckingham Gate, London SW1E 6LB, UK. Tel (0171) 233 5656.

Zentralstelle für Arbeitsvermittlung, Postfach 17 05 46, D-60079 Frankfurt, Germany. Tel (069) 71110; fax (069) 7111540.

German Embassy, 3 Belgrave Square, London SW1X 8PZ, UK. Tel (0171) 235 6281.

German Federation of Chambers of Commerce Deutscher Industrie- und Handelstag, Adenauerallee 148, Postfach 1446, D-53113 Bonn, Germany.

Allkauf Zentralverwaltung, Reyerhütte 51, D-41065 Mönchengladbach, Germany.

The Employment Service, Overseas Placing Unit, c/o Rockingham House, 123 West Street, Sheffield S1 4ER, UK. Tel (0114) 259651; fax (0114) 2596040.

Comparability Co-ordinator, Employment Department, Qualification and ITOs Branch, TSIE1, Room E603, Moorfoot, Sheffield S1 4PQ, UK. Tel: (0114) 2753275; fax (0114) 2758316.

USEFUL WORDS AND PHRASES

Abschlußprüfung	final examination.
Ausbildung	training, apprenticeship.
Ausbildungsbetreib	company which trains you.
Ausbildungsvergütung	payment for trainees.
Ausbildungsvertrag	training contract.
Auszubildende/	(female/male) trainee, apprentice.
Auszubildender	
Beruf	profession, job, trade.
Berufsschule	college where trainees acquire the theoretical skills for their trade.
Geselle	trained craftsman or tradesman (woman).
Gesellenbrief	certificate of completed training for craftspeople and tradespeople.
Handwerkskammer	chamber for trades and crafts.
Industrie- und Handelskammer	chamber of industry and commerce.
Kaufmannsgehilfenbrief	certificate of completed training in commercial or administrative careers.
Lehrling	trainee (outdated, now replaced by **Auszubildener/Auszubildende**, but still in common use.
Meister	master craftsperson.
Probezeit	trial period.
Zwischenprüfung	intermediate examination.

SUMMARY

● Training schemes are thorough and strictly regulated.

● If you want a career in administration or trade, the best bet is to train as a retail manager.

● Don't expect to get rich while training.

● An EU occupations information sheet will help prospective employers to assess your qualifications.

9
Skilled and Qualified Work

NURSING

For general and specialist nurses, it is comparatively easy to find employment in Germany. Both Ingo Fischer of the Zentralstelle für Arbeitsvermittlung, and Ian Foulstone of the Overseas Placing Unit, confirm this.

However, German language skills, especially spoken German, are essential, so go on a crash course before you apply.

There are several recruitment agencies for nursing staff, in Germany as well as overseas. However, you can also apply through the Zentralstelle für Arbeitsvermittlung in Frankfurt (or the Overseas Placing Unit, if you live in the UK). The state employment service is keen to recruit nurses from abroad, although the process may be a slow one.

The newspaper *Overseas Job Express*, as well as the German regional and national newspapers, sometimes carry situations vacant advertisements for nurses. If you want to work in a particular town, send on spec applications to the hospitals there.

BUILDING & CONSTRUCTION

Construction workers are actively recruited in Germany, and the government encourages unemployed people to retrain as bricklayers.

At present, the demand for construction workers greatly exceeds the supply. Chances are excellent if you are fully qualified in any of these occupations:

- Bricklayer

- Roofer

- Carpenter

- Plasterer

- Ceramic tiler

- Flooring specialist

If you lack the qualification, but have several years' experience, it is still worth trying.

Many building workers are recruited through German, British or Dutch agencies. Until recently, this was a legal minefield, as many agencies were not licensed by the German state, and construction workers who went to Germany with an unlicensed agency found themselves in a difficult situation.

There are still some risks, especially if you are hired as a contractor. Make sure that you are going with a bona fide agency or, better still, insist on knowing your employer's name and address before you sign on.

But there is another safe option: you can apply through the Zentralstelle für Arbeitsvermittlung (or the Overseas Placing Unit, if you live in the UK). As Germany actually needs construction workers, the state employment organisation is able and most willing to help.

COMPUTING

'German companies prefer well degree or higher degree qualified staff with at least two years' actual post university work experience,' says Brian Harris of OCC Computer Personnel.

He adds that the general trend is to employ foreign candidates only if they speak German fluently. 'Writing and reading skills seem to be less important. But the number of employers who accept English only is rapidly declining.'

He finds that candidates by and large have exaggerated salary expectations. 'It is true that gross salary levels are much higher than in the UK. But cost of living and tax level differentials erode the net gain. As a rule of thumb, if you are better off by more than 10 per cent in net terms you are doing well.'

Programmers with several years' experience can expect between DM10,000 and DM90,000 per month, and salaries tend to be highest in the big south German cities.

Brian Harris warns: 'British staff can expect the job market in German speaking Europe to get tougher in the future. Continental companies will expect British staff to compete on an equal footing with local people. This means that you must learn German to a high degree of proficiency. If a Brit has fluent German and a highly sought-after skill set, she or he will probably be able to find work.

British computing expertise, flexibility and innovative tradition make UK computing skills sought after.'

If you are a UK resident computer specialist, contact: Brian Harris, 108 Welsh Row, Nantwich, Cheshire W5 5EY, UK. Tel (01270) 627206; fax (01270) 629168.

It is also worth sending on spec letters to major computing companies in Germany, and studying the sits vac adverts in German daily newspapers, or in *Overseas Jobs Express.*

CATERING

There are many vacancies for hotel and restaurant personnel. Many, however, are for a limited period only, for example the summer months. Winter tourism is not particularly strong in Germany, although there are several skiing areas.

Catering is the employment sector where foreigners are least likely to encounter prejudice and discrimination. Indeed, a small restaurant may gain prestige by employing an Italian waiter and a French chef. Jobs which involve dealing with the public — receptionist, waiter/waitress etc — require good German, but kitchen staff and chambermaids can get by without.

For catering jobs, apply through the Zentralstelle für Arbeitsvermittlung in Frankfurt or (if you live in the UK) through the Overseas Placing Unit. Remember to apply several months before the season starts, as the process can be slow and bureaucratic.

TEACHING

The situation for teachers in Germany is difficult. During the '70s and '80s, too many teachers trained at German universities — far too many for the limited job market. For several years, 'Lehrerarbeitslosigkeit' (teachers' unemployment) was one of the most frequent words in the newspaper headlines.

Many qualified teachers retrained for other occupations, but a great number of them are still waiting for an opportunity to return to teaching which they regard as their true vocation. It is almost impossible for foreign teachers to penetrate this job market.

A visit to the Arbeitsamt may be disappointing: the consultant will probably tell you that there are more applicants than vacancies, and you are unlikely to receive an offer. Unless you have strong personal reasons for going to Germany, the best advice is: take your teaching skills to another country.

A small chance exists if you are specialising in technical subjects or science. For TEFL teachers who can teach business and banking English, there are some vacancies at private language colleges such as Inlingua. Most of them require their teaching staff to speak fluent German.

A helpful book which contains lists of German language colleges which are likely to have vacancies, complete with work conditions and job descriptions, is *Teaching English Abroad — Talk Your Way Around The World!* by Susan Griffith. Most jobs mentioned require business English, a BA degree, a TEFL certificate plus experience.

The Central Bureau for Educational Visits and Exchanges organises the language assistant scheme. English language assistants help teachers of English at German secondary schools. The main task is to improve the students' listening and speaking skills, teaching approximately twelve hours a week. The course duration is from September to June of each year.

Candidates should be native English speakers, between 20 and 30 years of age, and should have completed at least two years of an honours degree or diploma course, if possible in German. Payment is DM1,150 per month. Closing date for applications is December 1, the year before you want to go.

Qualified experienced English teachers can participate in an in-service teacher exchange programme, also organised by the Central Bureau.

Students and teachers resident in Northern Ireland should contact: The Central Bureau, 16 Malone Road, Belfast BT9 5BN. Tel (0232) 664418.

In Scotland: The Central Bureau, 3 Bruntsfield Crescent, Edinburgh EH10 4HD, UK. Tel (0131) 447 8022.

In Wales and England: The Central Bureau, Assistants Department, Seymour Mews House, Seymour Mews, London W1H 9PE, UK. Tel: (0171) 486 5101.

ENGINEERING

There are always vacancies for technicians and engineers, particularly in major cities. Payment is excellent. However, the days are over when every candidate could choose between several job offers. Openings for engineers without fluent German are becoming rare.

At present, there is demand for telecommunication engineers. One of the main employers is the Telekom section of the Deutsche Bundepost. Telekom pays less than other employers (which is why German telecommunications engineers prefer to apply with private companies) and sometimes runs recruitment campaigns which may include study sponsorship.

LAW

Every year, several young lawyers from France, Belgium, Luxembourg, the Netherlands, the UK, the US and the CIS participate in a ten month study visit with work experience in Germany.

The programme includes a two month course in German legal terminology in Tübingen, a five month course in Düsseldorf on the German legal system under the direction of the Ministry of Justice of Nordrhein-Westfalen (North Rhine Westphalia) and three months' work experience in an institution or firm of the participant's choice.

The Deutscher Akademischer Austauschdienst (DAAD, German Academic Exchange Service) pays the course fees, a contribution towards the travel expenses to Germany, and a grant for a living allowance.

Barristers, solicitors, practising lawyers and law teachers can apply. They should not be older than 32 and must have fluent German. The selection interview will be conducted in German.

DAAD programmes and scholarships change every year, depending on the available funds. The Young Lawyers Programme may not always take place.

For information and application forms, contact:

Deutscher Akademischer Austauschdienst, Kennedyallee 50, D-53134 Bonn, Germany. Tel (0228) 882-0; fax (0228) 882-444.

German Academic Exchange Service, 17, Bloomsbury Square, London WC1A 2LP, UK. Tel (0171) 404 4065; fax (0171) 430 2634.

German Academic Exchange Service, 950 Third Avenue, 19th Floor, New York, NY 10022, USA. Tel (0212) 758 1014; fax (0212) 755 5780.

Office Allemand d'Echanges Universitaires, 15 rue de Verneuil, F-75007 Paris, France. Tel (01) 42615857; fax (01) 42869442.

SUMMARY

● Spoken German is essential for nursing and preferred for computing staff and engineers.

● Foreigners are least likely to encounter prejudice in the catering sector.

● Few vacancies exist for teachers.

10
Making Your Languages Work

The majority of Germans speak and write basic English; those who have attended school up to the higher school leaving exam (Abitur) are quite fluent. Perfect English, however, is much in demand for secretaries, international trade staff, receptionists and managers.

Chances are excellent if you understand technical and scientific subjects and know the relevant terminology in both your mother tongue and in German.

Dictionaries cannot keep up to date with the rapid development of languages in this sector.

The computing, non-nuclear energy and engineering industries offer many vacancies. There are also opportunities for linguists, particularly for those specialising in the sciences, with universities and research centres.

Business English and French are also in demand; potential employers include the large banks, financial institutions, shipping agents, trade fair organisers, importers and exporters.

TAKE YOUR SKILLS TO THE EAST

Demand exists particularly in the eastern part of Germany, where, until quite recently, Russian was the first (and usually the only) foreign language studied.

Although many schools offered the opportunity to learn either English or French, few students chose them. After all, they were unlikely ever to deal with westerners for business or travel, so why bother to learn a language which would never be used?

Few eastern Germans can afford to study languages at evening classes, which used to be available and affordable for all, but after the collapse of the socialist system were scrapped for lack of funding.

Companies in the east who wish to export have to invest time and money in training their staff not only in marketing skills and export

73

regulations, but also in languages. If they can afford it, they even send their newly appointed export manager on a crash course to Brighton.

Others prefer to buy in marketing and linguistic expertise from the west, which may work out cheaper for them. This can be a chance for applicants from other countries, especially with English or French mother tongue and experience in international trade.

Remember, however, that wages in the east are low and that there is virtually no chance of finding secretarial or managerial employment without fluent German. In addition, this type of appointment tends to be for a limited period only, for example one year. Foreign experts are expected to train existing staff, then disappear.

WORKING AS A BILINGUAL SECRETARY

One of the few careers in Germany not regulated by a standard training scheme is that of a secretary. Anyone with some office experience and typing skills can call themselves a secretary.

However, most secretaries have either attended a secretarial college — usually a lengthy, expensive course at a private school — or they have trained in a related field, *eg* 'Bürokauffrau/Bürokaufmann' (that is the female/male version of office administrator), or 'Industriekauffrau/Industriekaufmann' (industrial manager).

Bilingual secretaries who trained in their native country and have a good command of German can adapt easily in most cases. What they are likely to find rather difficult at first, however, is taking phone calls.

Understanding what someone says rapidly in the accent of a different region of Germany, without seeing their facial expression or gestures, possibly on a poor line, is quite a job. Keep calm, ask them to repeat the information, to spell out names.

If you don't want to admit that you cannot understand what they say, blame the poor phone connection!

You will also have to get used to the German keyboard. It is similar to the UK keyboard, but the keys for y and z are exchanged. This demands enormous concentration and will slow down your typing speed for the first weeks.

Grading

There are three levels of bilingual secretaries:
1. 'Fremdsprachliche Sekretärin': reasonable typing skills, and enough knowledge of a language to type a simple business letter.

2. 'Fremdsprachensekretärin': excellent secretarial skills, including good typing speed, shorthand, experience, and organisation skills. Reasonable knowledge of the language — enough for composing own letters and making business related phone-calls.

3. 'Fremdsprachenkorrespondentin': reasonable secretarial skills, including good typing speed, but not necessarily shorthand. Excellent language skills — ability to handle all the company's foreign correspondence and phone calls on their own, as well as business related translations from and into the foreign language.

Obtain a certificate

If you don't already have a bilingual secretarial qualification, contact a German Industrie- und Handelskammer (the chamber of commerce equivalent, IHK for short).

Chambers of commerce arrange examinations twice a year to evaluate skills. These examinations cost DM350 (DM730 if you want to have your secretarial skills as well as your linguistic skills examined). They are not obligatory, but increase the chances of finding a good position. The difficulty of the tests is often under-rated, and examinations at which one in four candidates fails are no exception.

To get addresses of German chambers of commerce which conduct examinations, you can write to the German chamber of commerce in your native country, if there is one, or to the Deutscher Industrie- und Handelstag.

The exams are not the same nationwide — in northern Germany they are considered to be easier than in the south, and in Bavaria the chambers of commerce demand most from their candidates.

Sample examination papers are usually available to enable candidates to evaluate their skills before they sit for the exams.

The subjects for foreign bilingual secretaries who are tested in German are:

● General knowledge of business in Germany (functions of the chambers of commerce, register of companies, retail, wholesale, franchising, commercial travellers etc)

● Company law and structure (limited companies, co-operatives, buying, distribution, customer service, advertising, accounts, administration etc)

- Post (letter and parcel post, telecommunications, money transactions such as postal orders)

- Banking and finance (services supplied by banks, sorting codes, types of accounts, credit procedure, credit cards, cash dispensers, investment advice, stock market, stocks and shares, bonds)

- Distribution (marketing, market research, consumer surveys, sales promotion, PR, target groups, advertising campaigns)

- Enquiries and tenders (solicited and unsolicited offers etc)

- Orders (mail order, sale or return, regular orders etc)

The IHK Karlsruhe, for example, supplies sample examination papers which comprise the following elements:

- a dictation about economic difficulties in Singapore

- writing a business letter about strategies to increase sales of wooden toys

- writing a business letter about licensing agreements for power-transmission systems

- a translation of minutes of a meeting about the conditions for the termination of an agency agreement

- a translation of a checklist for launching a business enterprise.

To be admitted to the exams, you have to fulfil one of the following conditions:

- have completed two to three year training scheme and obtained a chamber of commerce certificate plus two years' experience, all in an occupation related to bilingual secretarial work (*eg* office administration).

- have completed two to three year training scheme and obtained a chamber of commerce certificate, plus one year's experience, all in an occupation related to bilingual secretarial work, plus O or A level equivalent education

- completed a course at business college plus one year's office work experience

- higher education (Abitur) plus one year's office work experience

- O-level equivalent plus four years' office work experience

- six years' work experience in an office environment

If you don't fulfil any of the above conditions, you may apply for an exception, but have to prove first that you are likely to possess the necessary skills.

'Everyone who fulfils these conditions can participate in a Chamber of Commerce Language examination,' explains Frau Grothe-Schmidt, who is in charge of language exams at the IHK Karlsruhe.

'The contents of the exams are the same for foreign nationals and for Germans, but the tested language for foreigners is German.'

Chambers of commerce examine only bilingual secretaries who are specialising in business German — the area in which bilingual secretaries are employed most frequently. Occasionally, there are also vacancies for technical or political bilingual secretaries, but the chambers don't arrange exams for these.

TRANSLATING AND INTERPRETING

The subject which is most in demand, and best paid, is technology, followed by sciences, law and business. Political translators are reasonably well paid, but literary translators are sometimes offered little more than typists.

Everyone can call themselves Übersetzer (translator) or Dolmetscher (interpreter). However, you are more likely to find employment if you possess a recognised qualification, for example:

- a language degree (Diplom) from a German university or Fachhochschule. Graduates put the word Diplom in front of their qualification, ie Diplomübersetzer/Diplomübersetzerin or Diplomdolmetscher/Diplomdolmetscherin. University graduates often specialise in one of the following subjects: technology, sciences, business, law, politics, literature

- a translator's degree from a university in your native country

- a translator's diploma from a national organisation in your native country, such as the Institute of Linguists in the UK

- a degree equivalent translator's diploma issued after examination by a chamber of commerce in Germany. This allows you to put 'Staatlich anerkannt' in front of your qualification, *ie* Staatlich anerkannte Übersetzerin/Staatlich anerkannter Übersetzer or Staatlich anerkannte Dolmetscherin/Staatlich anerkannter Dolmetscher. Chambers of commerce issue qualification certificates only for translators and interpreters who specialise in business. Some chambers of commerce examine only translators. The examination costs DM450.

- a degree equivalent translator's diploma issued after examination by a Kultusministerium (ministry of education and the arts of a Bundesland) in Germany. This allows you to put 'Staatlich geprüft' in front of your qualification, *ie* Staatlich geprüfte Übersetzerin/Staatlich geprüfter Übersetzer or Staatlich geprüfte Dolmetscherin/Staatlich geprüfter Dolmetscher. A Kultusministerium issues qualification certificates only for translators and interpreters who specialise in politics. If you are living in Germany, contact the Kultusministerium of your Bundesland; if you are still in your home country, contact the German embassy for initial information. See p138 for useful addresses.

If you possess any of the above qualifications, you can increase your professional standing by becoming 'vereidigt'. This means that you are sworn in at a court and can then interpret court proceedings and translate statements. Courts often use the services of translators and interpreters who are vereidigt, and they pay well.

Many Germans are vereidigt for English or French, but if you are qualified in a less common language and live in a big city, you could earn a nice amount of extra money. Enquire at your local Amtsgericht (county court).

SUMMARY

- Understanding of technical and scientific subjects and the ability to translate the terminology are much in demand.

- Fluent, unflappable bilingual secretaries with recognised qualifications have a good chance of employment.

- You can better your chances by obtaining a recognised German qualification.

11
Vacation and Temporary Work

As in many comparatively wealthy countries, casual work is easy to find for foreigners who are willing to work hard, despite the increasing unemployment rate. The prospects are better in the west than in the east, where unemployment is high.

If you are willing to take on any type of work, you can work your way across Germany for a year. Most jobs are given to people who apply on the spot, so you may want to take the plunge and just go there. The Zentralstelle für Arbeitsvermittlung can help casual workers who are willing to stay several weeks or months in one job, particularly for seasonal work.

Write for a form to: Zentralstelle für Arbeitsvermittlung, Postfach 170545, D-60079 Frankfurt. Tel (069) 7111-0; fax (069) 7111-540.

GRAPE AND FRUIT HARVESTING

Grape harvesting is popular and well paid on a daily or hourly rate — no work and no payment in heavy rain! Forget the picture post-card image of pretty girls in dirndls, and get used to the idea of mostly middle aged or retired, hard working people in anoraks and wellingtons.

In Germany, grapes need longer to ripen than in other countries, and the harvest begins later, usually in October. It can last until December for the famous 'Eiswein'. Workers need basic German only (many come from other countries, eg Poland), but the hard physical labour in cold unpleasant weather requires good health.

Women do the picking, men carry the buckets. Workers get cold fingers, and at the same time grow hot and sticky with grape juice all over despite wearing warm trousers, padded jacket, wellingtons, headscarf/hat and plastic gloves. Workers are usually collected in a minibus.

Best chances are in the major wine growing areas where the demand for workers exceeds the number of housewives and students available for seasonal work. Most vineyards are concentrated in the south west and along the rivers Rhein (Rhine) and Mosel (Moselle). There is also some casual work in the vineyards outside the harvesting season, but vacancies are limited.

Wine growers are unlikely to consider applications from abroad; you will have to take the risk and go to Germany. If you arrive before the main season starts, the Arbeitsamt may be able to find work. But you can also phone the wine growers to offer your services.

To find out about German grapes and where they are grown, contact: German Wine Information Service, Chelsea Chambers, 262a Fulham Road, London SW10 9EL, UK. Tel (0181) 3763329; fax (0181) 3517563.

However, the German Wine Information Service is only involved in the promotion of the product; it cannot help you find a job. But it may be able to supply you with addresses.

Harvesting fruit is a well paid job for those who don't mind high ladders, cold fingers, and lots of spiders. Basic German only is required. July is the season for picking cherries, and September for apples. Try the rural areas in the north near Hamburg, Steinkirchen, Jork, Horneburg and Stade, or the region south of Frankfurt.

CHAMBERMAIDS

Jobs for 'Zimmermädchen' are available in tourist areas and in summer only, and basic language skills are required. The North Sea coast, the Black Forest and the Bavarian Alps are the regions with the most potential, but other tourist areas are also worth trying.

A commitment for two to three months in summer is usually required. Net wages are likely to be around DM400-500 per month plus board and lodging, or around DM800 per month without board and lodging. Larger hotels tend to pay more than smaller ones. If you are going to a major city where the rents are enormous, the former is definitely preferable! A good book to have is *Summer Jobs Abroad* which lists many hotels with their precise requirements for temp staff, including conditions of work and pay.

WAITER/WAITRESS

Employment for a Kellner (male) or a Kellnerin (female) can be found in restaurants, pubs, beergardens and Weinstuben: the best time for this type of work is June to September in tourism areas. Another season is Fasnacht or Karneval, the traditional carnival weeks celebrated in February in the south and along the river Rhein (Rhine). If you are looking for just one week's work, go end of September to the Oktoberfest in München (Munich) or other big towns and cities.

Applicants stand a better chance if they've had some waitressing experience in their home country, and speak German.

Don't even attempt to find a vacancy in a town or city which has a university or polytechnic — there are long waiting lists of students who want to work in pubs to finance their studies.

Again, *Summer Jobs Abroad* contains addresses and information. Make sure you have the latest issue — the guide appears annually.

BUILDING AND CONSTRUCTION

This is hard and well paid work. You need some basic German. The demand fluctuates, depending on the economic situation and the weather, and it may not be possible to find legal short term opportunities. Contact the builders listed in the yellow pages.

FAST FOOD

You can find a job easily — just walk in and ask to speak to the manager. If the first fast food restaurant doesn't have a vacancy, the second probably has. Your chances are even better if you have fast food experience, or if you can convince the manager that you will be available for more than a few weeks.

Only basic German is required: chips are called 'Pommes Frites', but hamburgers are 'Hamburger'. The main disadvantage is the lousy pay — perhaps just enough to survive if you share a room with several others in a hostel. If you are prepared to stay for several months, you may even get promotion and become shift manager (and earn slightly more).

TOWN AND MUSEUM GUIDES

Major tourist attractions hire foreign language guides. Chances are reasonable for those with a degree in arts or history who are available for the whole season.

The Volkshochschule (Adult Education Centre) in Trier runs a course for town guides. Only applicants who have attended the course and passed the exam can apply for a guide job in Trier. Elsewhere, no specific qualifications are required.

Although smart dress is required for this type of job, avoid high heels — you'll be standing and walking all day. Payment is modest.

CLEANING

This is a reasonably well paid task, usually performed in the evenings. Apply for a job with one of the cleaning businesses which advertise in the local papers. Basic German is required. Take several character references with you, *eg* from your vicar, from a former employer, from your school's headmaster. Cleaning businesses make a point of investigating their staff's character, and may be hesitant to employ foreigners without references.

ROWING BOAT HIRE

Try tourist areas at lakes. Payment is modest, but the work can be pleasant and you'll acquire a nice sun tan. Staff must be available whole season (May - September) and speak German. Applicants are often hired as a boy-and-girl team: the boy because of his physical strength, the girl because of her good looks to attract customers. This is a good job opportunity for young couples. Make sure, however, that you receive payment on rainy days when there is no business!

TRADE FAIR HOSTESS

The work is pleasant, prestigious and well paid, *eg* handing out brochures, serving coffee and wine. Wear a suit or skirt and blouse — avoid high heels, as the job involves standing.

Fluent German is essential; additional languages are a great advantage. Jobs are available almost exclusively to young, smart looking women.

Register with the Messerarbeitsvermittlung (trade fair employment service), a department of the Arbeitsamt. There is a Messerarbeitsvermittlung in every city where large trade fairs are being held.

Staff are usually hired for the duration of the trade fair. You cannot work anywhere for more than a week or two, but if you want to see a lot of Germany, the job is ideal: work at the IGEDO in Düsseldorf, at the Modewoche in München, at the ANUGA in Frankfurt.

People are also required for building and taking down the exhibition stalls. Strong males are preferred here. Again, contact the Messerarbeitsvermittlung.

OFFICE AND RETAIL STAFF

Employing temporary office staff is not yet as common in Germany as it is in other countries. In large cities you will find agencies for temporary secretaries. These agencies are called Zeitarbeitsvermitt-lung and they advertise in the regional daily press. There are vacancies during the summer months, especially in the cities. However, you must have experience in office or secretarial work and speak and write German fluently.

In the weeks before Christmas, additional retail staff is required as cashiers, to wrap parcels etc. Knowledge of German is necessary. Contact the local Arbeitsamt or phone the personnel department of the large department stores.

SUMMARY

- Flexibility and willingness to work hard are the keys to most temporary jobs.

- The better your German, the more opportunities will be open to you.

- Many temp jobs are seasonal.

- You can apply to prospective employers directly, or use the help of the Arbeitsamt.

12
Voluntary and Unpaid Work

If your main motivation for working in Germany is to gain experience in a new field, to 'get away from it all', or to widen your horizon, and if you don't care much about your income and living standard, then voluntary work could be the right option.

Several organisations offer postings in Germany. Food and accommodation are usually provided. Some organisations pay pocket money, others expect volunteers to contribute towards the expenses of the project.

FINDING THE RIGHT ORGANISATION

Aktion Sühnezeichen
The aims of the organisation are to preserve peace and protect minorities; projects include working with and for travelling people or refugees.

Volunteers receive free board and lodging, as well as pocket money of up to DM250 per month.

Applicants must be at least 18 years old before they can take up the work, and must commit themselves for 18 months. Work hours per week depend on the project.

'Everyone who can identify with our aims can apply', explains office manager Jens Pohl.

All applicants receive information brochures and forms to fill in, and are asked to participate in a seminar, during which the selection is being made. 'Interviews and discussions will show if candidates are suitable to work with us. It is not necessary to belong to a particular religious group.'

He adds: 'Most of our volunteers are placed with social work projects. If applicants have previous social work experience, they are at an advantage. In any case, we would ask applicants to serve a work experience period at a social institution in their home country before committing themselves for 18 months.'

Write to: Aktion Sühnezeichen Friedensdienste e.V., Postfach 154, D-10365 Berlin, Germany. Tel (030) 55190310; fax (030) 55190376.

Christlicher Friedensdienst

Young people who are looking for unpaid work experience of three to four weeks can participate in work camps.

Recent projects have included social work with children, explaining different cultures with the help of games, songs and recipes to school children in an area of Berlin where racism is strong, and restoring peace monuments. Nature preservation projects involve building dry stone walls, mowing meadows, carrying away the hay, building small ponds and nesting-boxes.

The age limit for participants from abroad is 18-26 years. Accommodation will be provided, explains Ursula Pohl of Christlicher Friedensdienst. 'But it is basic, usually in dormitories. The meals are basic, too, arranged and cooked by the group themselves.'

Christlicher Friedensdienst is a Christian organisation, but participants need not belong to a particular religious group. 'We believe that every candidate is suitable who is able to live and work in a group of between ten and twenty people,' says Ursula Pohl. She points out that the projects are suitable for handicapped people.

Two detailed programmes are available, one for projects in Germany and one for projects in other countries.

In addition, Christlicher Friedensdienst is looking for camp leaders in Germany. These need to have team leadership experience, and should ideally have completed relevant studies or training schemes. Work includes introducing projects, preparing camps, working with multi-cultural groups, administration and finance. Camp leaders are paid DM200 plus expenses.

Write to: CFD, Christlicher Friedensdienst, Rendelerstr. 9-11, D-60385 Frankfurt, Germany. Tel (069) 459072; fax (069) 461213.

Applicants from the UK can apply via the British branch: Christian Movement for Peace, 186 St. Paul's Road, Balsall Heath, Birmingham B12 8LZ, UK. Tel (0121) 4465704; fax (0121) 4464060.

Freiwilliges Soziales Jahr

If you are prepared to give one year of your life to help others, in return for board, lodging, pocket money and experience, you can apply to a variety of organisations for social work.

Initially, the Freiwilliges Soziales Jahr (FSJ) was organised by the churches in the '50s, often to help children in refugee camps. Today, typical placements are in hospitals, old people's homes, children's homes, and homes for the physically or mentally handicapped. Since 1963 the German Red Cross and other non-religious organisations and charities have also offered FSJ placements.

Volunteers must sincerely wish to help by giving human warmth and understanding, as well as by physical work. They are laypeople, but receive instructions and training from qualified staff.

Because of the acute shortage of nurses, placements in hospitals are easy to find. About ten per cent of volunteers are men.

Applicants must be between seventeen and twenty-five years, fit and healthy. Many Germans use it as a gap year between school and university. Most placements begin in August, September and October, and it is advisable to apply in spring. However, some last minute vacancies can arise when accepted volunteers withdraw because they have been awarded a university place at short notice.

Nobody can do more than one FSJ. A few placements are available which take only six months or less, but the organisers tend to take only local volunteers for these and provide no accommodation.

About DM300 pocket money is paid per month. In addition, accommodation (usually in twin bedded rooms), canteen meals and uniforms or work clothes are provided.

ABC zum Diakonischen Jahr is a brochure with detailed information, and contact addresses of institutions which accept volunteers, which is available from: Arbeitskreis Freiwillige Soziale Dienste (an organisation of the protestant church), Stafflenbergstr. 76, D-70184 Stuttgart, Germany. Tel (0711) 2159-0; fax (0711) 2159-288.

Main organisers for Freiwilliges Soziales Jahr include:

Arbeiterwohlfahrt (Workers' Charity), Oppelner Str. 130, D-53119 Bonn, Germany.

Bund der Deutschen Katholischen Jugend (Catholic Youth Association), Carl-Mosters-Platz 1, D-40477 Düsseldorf, Germany.

Deutsches Rotes Kreuz (German Red Cross), Friedrich-Ebert-Allee 71, D-53113 Bonn, Germany.

Regional organisers (mostly linked to the church) include:

Diakonisches Werk Württemberg, Diakonisches Jahr, Postfach 10 11 51, D-70191 Stuttgart, Germany.

Diakonisches Werk Oldenburg, Freiwilliges Soziales Jahr, Gottorpstr. 23, D-26122 Oldenburg, Germany.

Amt für Jugendarbeit Baden, Freiwillige Soziale Dienste, Vorholzstr. 7, D-76137 Karlsruhe, Germany.

Diakonisches Werk Bremen, Freiwillige Soziale Dienste, Blumenthalstr. 10/11, D-28209 Bremen, Germany.

Diakonisches Werk, Hessen und Nassau, Freiwillige Soziale Dienste, Ederstr. 12, D-60486 Frankfurt, Germany.

Diakonisches Werk, Berlin-Brandenburg, Diakonisches Jahr, Schönhauser Allee 141, D-10437 Berlin, Germany.

Diakonisches Jahr der Evangelischen Kirche von Westfalen, Melcherstr. 57, D-48149 Münster, Germany.

Christen in der Offensive, Diakonisches Jahr, Postfach 1220, D-64385 Reichelsheim/Odenwald, Germany.

Diakonisches Werk der Ev.-Luth. Landeskirche Sachsens e.V., Freiwilliges Soziales Jahr, Obere Bergstr. 1, D-01445 Radebeul, Germany.

Diakonisches Werk in der Kirchenprovinz Sachsens e.V., Freiwilliges Soziales Jahr, Mittagstr. 5, D-39124 Magdeburg, Germany.

Diakonisches Werk der Evang. Kirche in Thüringen e.V., Freiwilliges Soziales Jahr, Am Ofenstein 9, D-99817 Eisenach, Germany.

Diakonisches Werk in der Pommerschen Evang. Kirche e.V., Rudolf-Petershagen-Allee 38, Haus IV, D-17489 Greifswald, Germany.

Diakonisches Werk der Ev.-Luth. Landeskirche Mecklenburgs e.V., Freiwilliges Soziales Jahrn, Körnerstr. 19, D-19055 Schwerin, Germany.

Collegium Augustinum Philadelphischer Ring e.V., Stiftsbogen 74, D-81375 München, Germany.

Gemeindejugendwerk, Freiwilliges Soziales Jahn, Rennbahnstr. 115b, D-22111 Hamburg, Germany.

CHECKLIST

Before committing yourself, ask the following questions:

● Do I want to help people?

● Am I willing to do physically and mentally strenuous work?

● Am I interested in social/environmental work?

● Can I identify with the organisation's aims?

● Can I live for the required period under basic conditions, usually with shared accommodation?

● Can I afford to pay for the return ticket?

● Do I have financial commitments which I cannot meet from the pocket money?

● Do my family support my plans?

● For how long am I available?

● How does the voluntary work fit in with my career plans?

GETTING UNPAID WORK EXPERIENCE

If you have long term career plans, and money is no object in the short term, you can apply for unpaid work experience placements with German companies.

Use an agency

Either approach the companies of your choice directly, or use the services of an agency. One agency which specialises in finding work experiences across the European borders is European Affairs.

Manager Andy Kevern explains that the company charges for its services: 'How much we charge depends on how obscure the requests are. Some placements are easier to find than others. The fee for a one month placement for a college student or graduate in the retail sector would be £50. But there is no sector in which we wouldn't attempt to find a placement.'

In addition, candidates have to find the resources for a return ticket and board and lodging. Andy Kevern says: 'We can help in finding low cost accommodation, for example staying with a family, full board.'

The company, founded in 1992, deals mostly with language holidays. Its operations can be compared with a special interest travel agency. France and the UK were the first countries they covered for work experiences.

Their services are popular with college students whose curriculum requires a particular type of work experience.

Unpaid work placements could also be helpful for job hunters who need a kick start in Germany. One month could be used to gain experience, to acquire the terminology of the trade, and to add the name of a reputable German company to the CV.

Write to: Caroline and Andy Kevern, European Affairs, 10 Buckley Road, St. Neots, Cambridgeshire PE19 2TR, UK.

CHECKLIST

● Do I have precise, long term career plans?

● Am I able, and willing, to invest in a work placement?

● How much will it cost me — food, accommodation, travel, agency fee?

● Can I find a sponsor?

● What type of company (industry sector, size) would suit my requirements best?

● What type of work would I want to do?

● What do I hope to learn during the work placement?

● How much time can I invest in a work placement?

● Do I intend to return to my home country after the work placement, or do I intend to stay and find a paid-for job?

● How can I utilise my work experience time to build up contacts which may lead to a job?

13
Spending a Year Au Pair

.Working conditions for au pairs have been standardised for many European states. An au pair usually does five hours per day household and child care work for pocket money, has one full day off per week, and must have the opportunity to attend language classes, as well as religious services if he or she wishes. In addition, an au pair may be expected to babysit for up to two nights a week. She should have her own, lockable room.

An au pair's position is somewhere between a family member and paid staff. Where the contract does not outline rights and duties, this 'in between' situation can lead to wrong expectations: parents expecting full time labour, and au pairs expecting full time social life.

By using the services of a professional au pair agency, you can make sure that the family has been interviewed and a proper contract drawn up.

Debbie Bushell of the Solihull Au Pair & Nanny Agency, which places au pairs in Germany, explains: 'The working hours of an au pair in Germany appear to be the same as in England, about 30-35 hours per week, and they receive approximately £30 plus bed and board.'

Accommodation is in single rooms, and the spare time must be arranged in a way which allows the au pair to attend language courses.

One year is the normal period of stay, although there are sometimes openings for two to six months. 'Most of our agents in Germany will only accept applicants who can stay for six months or longer', says Debbie Bushell.

Sandra Clark of South Eastern Au Pair Bureau confirms: 'Six months is the minimum. Only occasionally an employer asks for a summer au pair for three months.'

Chances to find a placement are excellent: 'There seem to be a lot of vacancies for au pairs in Germany', says Debbie Bushell. 'We have many applicants, but we are always asked for even more au pairs than we have on our books!'

Both male and female candidates can apply for au pair placements. 'Personally, I think that men and women can be equally good at au pairing, but it seems that most people prefer females, probably because it is still viewed as a female role.'

Occasionally, a family may ask specifically for a male. 'For example, a single mother with a couple of school-aged boys. She may want a male presence in the house, someone who can play football with the boys, and so on.'

WHAT THE JOB INVOLVES

The average duties of an au pair can include looking after the children, supervising their homework, preparing meals for them, washing their clothes, as well as general household duties such as light cleaning and ironing.

Normally, an au pair should not be required to do heavy cleaning — certainly not if other household staff is employed.

There are some au pair positions which do not involve looking after children, but a lot of ironing, washing, cooking and cleaning.

Perfect applicants

The ideal applicant can cook, has experience with children and of housework, and at least basic German.

Sometimes, candidates are interested in au pairing, but are not suitable, especially those who have never had contact with children or housework. 'Such as, for example, a girl who has spent her life at boarding school, whose family had servants at home who did all the work, with no younger brother and sisters, who never had to earn her pocket money by baby sitting,' says Sandra Clark.

'If they have never been exposed to housework and babysitting, and they are suddenly thrown in at the deep end, they experience a shock, which is natural.'

She adds: 'We asks candidates in the application form if they can cook, wash, iron, feed babies, etc. If they tick no for all those questions, we don't take them on. The employers would simply not accept them.'

Basic German helps. 'Some employers speak English and are happy to take an au pair who has not learnt German yet,' says Sandra Clark. 'But remember that you are not spending all your time with the family. You want to go out and have your own social life.

For your own benefit, learn some German before you go out there, otherwise you may feel isolated at times.'

With your application, you should include two passport photographs which show you smiling. Additional photos which show you with happy children are very persuasive.

It appears that some placements are better than others. What you get is the luck of the draw. But a good agency will screen all families carefully, and match the family's interests with the au pair's.

WHAT YOU WILL GAIN

- You can experience life in Germany first hand.

- One year in Germany will cost you very little: you may well break even.

- Sometimes you will spend holidays with the family in exotic locations.

- You may live in luxurious surroundings.

- You have your own room and can thus retain some privacy.

- Your German will improve rapidly.

- You can widen your horizon.

- Au pairing will help your long term career plans, especially if you plan to work with children, in the domestic sector or with languages.

- You will become more tolerant of other ways of life.

- You will acquire or improve household skills.

- You may make friends for a lifetime.

WHAT MIGHT CAUSE YOU PROBLEMS

- The au pair is given too much work, sometimes 48 hours or more, perhaps because the employer who has never done housework tends to underestimate the time needed for certain tasks.

- The children are spoilt brats determined to make the au pair's life hell, and the parents don't interfere.

- The au pair is used to replace a full time cleaner or cook.

- The man of the house harasses the au pair sexually, and the au pair does not know how to deal with the situation (do you tell the wife? She may blame the au pair rather than the husband!)

- The wife feels guilty for not being able to cope with the housework on her own and is insecure about how to treat the au pair.

- The employers are very strict about your social life: no visitors, no boyfriends, no staying out later than 10pm.

- Your employer expects perfection in everything, and you just can't do anything right.

- Your employers enjoy power and make you feel it. They would enjoy owning slaves or at least employing lots of domestic staff but cannot afford it. They employ an au pair to feel like powerful important people.

- You don't know the language enough to make friends and feel lonely, isolated and homesick.

IS IT RIGHT FOR YOU?

However, these difficulties are not the norm! Most au pair placements are happy and beneficial for both sides. Give yourself a few weeks to settle in before you decide that the placement isn't right for you.

It is a good idea to apply through an agency which is either based in Germany or has local agents. Should difficulties arise, the agent will help sort them out, or arrange another placement.

'Applicants must be aware of what will be required from them', says Debbie Bushell. 'Be sure that you are willing to make this commitment. Remember that au pairs are there to help the families, and that give and take is required on both sides.'

CHECK YOUR MOTIVATION

- Can I adapt easily to new surroundings?

- Do I honestly like children?

- Do I have experience in looking after small children (younger siblings etc)?

- If yes, did I enjoy it?

- If I have little experience, am I sure I will like it?

- Do I enjoy housework?

- Do I have household skills, such as cooking and ironing?

- Can I take orders from parents who may be less educated and not much older than myself?

- Do I like responsibility?

- Am I a clean, tidy, well organised person?

- Is my German good enough to understand instructions, and to make myself understood to children?

- Is it good enough to get by on my own in my spare time?

- How will au pairing fit in with my overall career plans?

- How long do I want to stay? Do I really want to commit myself for so long?

- Can I afford one year without proper income?

- Do I have dependants or older family members who might require my help and presence?

FINDING A PLACEMENT

The book *Summer Jobs Abroad*, edited by David Woodworth, contains addresses of agencies as well as of parents looking for au pairs. A new issue is published every year.

Au Pair & Nanny Jobs Worldwide is a book in the *Get Up and Go Guides* series which gives lots of practical information.

you have just taken up your new job and can't get away from work. It is a good idea to start your official life in Germany one week before you start working, to cope with the red tape. The bureaucratic route takes time.

FINDING ACCOMMODATION

Jobhunters find that most employers are reluctant to give jobs — even temporary work — to anyone without a 'fester Wohnsitz' (permanent address) in Germany. It helps to rent a flat or a room as soon as you arrive in the town of your choice, even before you start looking for work.

But finding accommodation in Germany is even more difficult than finding a job. Unless you are going to a very rural area, or are prepared to pay horrendous hotel bills, you'll need to invest considerable time in the search. In some cities — Berlin and München in particular — flat-hunting becomes a full time occupation for several weeks or months.

Even in smaller towns, there are often as many as one hundred applicants for a reasonably priced flat.

Landlords can afford to make incredible demands — *eg* that the tenants do two hours' gardening or baby sitting per day in addition to paying the huge rent. There are even cases of tenants granting sexual favours on a regular basis.

Most people in Germany live in rented accommodation. Rents are a little lower in Germany than they are in the UK, but they are going up rapidly. In addition, tenants are responsible for any repairs for which in the UK the landlord would pay, and have to redecorate the property completely when they move out.

Buy the local newspaper, probably a daily which carries a classified section once a week. You'll notice that the 'Mietgesuche' (accommodation wanted) columns take up ten times as much space as the 'Zu vermieten' (accommodation offered).

Don't be surprised if nobody answers the phone when you ring the number printed in a classified advertisement. Demand may be such that by 5am on publication day the landlady has received the first 40 phone calls! At 5.30 am she may pick up the receiver only to say the single word 'vergeben' (gone), and put it down again. By 7am she is likely to unplug the phone.

If you are lucky enough to be invited to view a flat, wear a suit and try to look as respectable as possible. Take a cheque with you — offer to pay the deposit immediately.

Sometimes it's the present tenants who are looking for successors ('Nachmieter'). In return for recommending you to the landlord, they will demand a considerable sum of money (Ablöse). Demanding this sort of payment is against the law and is therefore disguised as compensation for furniture left behind. Don't be surprised if the present tenant suggests that you pay £1,000 for a defective washing machine. It's the bribe they expect.

Alternatively, you may use the services of a Makler (agent). They usually charge a fee equivalent to two months' rent, and the properties they have to let are likely to be expensive. Agents, too, have long waiting lists of prospective tenants. They are not allowed to charge for registration; you pay them only for their success.

Placing your own advert

Placing your own classified advertisement in the local newspaper is usually the best way. Describe yourself as a professional, quiet, non-smoking woman without pets (or whatever).

State what type of work you do or who you work for if you've got a job already. Explain what size of flat you want, the preferred location, and the rent you're willing to pay. Always give a telephone number. If you don't have a phone, ask a friend to take messages, and return the call the same day.

Landlords who are tired of telephone terror caused by advertising a flat, prefer answering adverts themselves. Women tend to get more offers — perhaps because they are thought to be tidier and quieter, but there may be a few indecent proposals.

If you've got a job already, ask your employers to place an advert. 'We are looking for a flat for our secretary . . .' This increases your chances, because in the eyes of a German landlord you are 'seriös' (respectable) if your company advertises for you. However, the resulting offers may be slightly overpriced.

The most effective heading for a flat wanted advert is 'Belohnung' (reward). Although demanding bribes is illegal, offering bribes is not! The amount offered varies, usually one month's rent; compare other advertisements. That's still cheaper than using a Makler. If you feel put off by these practices, think of an original, non-monetary reward. One flat hunter had astonishing success by offering a home-baked apple cake!

Put up cards with flat wanted/reward offered requests in shops and pubs frequented by students. There is no charge for this.

Find out if your town has a 'Mitwohnzentrale'. This means 'accommodation share centre', a small business agency charging much lower fees than normal agents. Mitwohnzentralen specialize in finding tenants for flatshares, and in sub-letting flats in the absence of the main tenant.

A tenant going abroad for three weeks contacts the Mitwohnzentrale, which finds a suitable sub-tenant, takes up references etc, and gives advice on a sub-letting contract. The main tenants know that their plants will be watered, the cats fed, the post forwarded, the rooms heated, and that burglars will be deterred. The sub-tenant gets accommodation at a reasonable price, paying only the rent and the bills, or even less.

Mitwohnzentralen are ideal if you need temporary accommodation until you find something permanent, or if you want to spend only a few weeks in each town.

In some tourist areas, it is possible to rent holiday accommodation at reasonable prices during winter. During the summer vacation, you may be able to obtain a room in a 'Studentenwohnheim' (university hall).

Youth hostels

Other possibilities include the Christlicher Verein junger Menschen (CVJM = YMCA) and Jugendherbergen (youth hostels).

Membership of the youth hostel organisation is especially helpful if you plan to work your way across Germany or need temporary accommodation for a few days only. There are around 700 Jugendherbergen, some right in the middle of towns, others in romantic old castles, which have developed into international meeting places. A list of hostels can be obtained for DM6.50.

Accommodation is in bedrooms with two to six beds, separate for men and women. Most youth hostels are open until 10pm — later in large cities.

If you want to stay in a Jugendherberge, you need a membership card (apply to your own country's youth hostel association). Alternatively, you can buy an international guest card at most hostels.

It is advisable to book in advance in writing. There is no age limit except in Bavaria, where visitors must be under 27 years.

Deutsches Jugendherbergswerk, Hauptverband e.V., Bismarckstr. 8, Postfach 20, D-32754 Detmold, Germany. Tel (052 31) 74010; fax (0531) 640149.

CVJM Gesamtverband Deutschland, Postfach 410149, Im Druseltal 8, D-34131 Kassel-Wilhelmshöhe, Germany.

In general your chances of finding accommodation at a reasonable price will increase the further away you get from large cities and university towns. Bear in mind that Germans describe a flat not by stating the number of bedrooms, but by counting all rooms excluding kitchen and bath.

USEFUL WORDS AND PHRASES

Ablöse	payment to former tenant.
Belohnung	reward.
Schlafsaal	dormitory.
Drei-Zimmer-Wohnung (3 Zi Whg)	flat with three rooms plus bath and kitchen.
Haus	house.
Jugendherberge	youth hostel.
Kaltmiete	rent excluding bills.
Kaution	deposit.
Mieter/Mieterin	tenant.
möbliert	furnished.
Nachmieter gesucht	successor wanted (willing to pay Ablöse to present tenant).
Nebenkosten (NK)	bills.
Nichtraucher/Nichtraucherin (NR)	non smoker.
Provision	agent's fee.
ruhig	quiet (used for flats and tenants alike).
Studentenwohnheim	university hall.
teilmöbliert	part furnished.
unmöbliert	unfurnished.
Untermieter/Untermieterin	sub-tenant.
Vereinbarung (VB)	price negotiable.
Vermieter/Vermieterin	landlord, landlady.
Wohngemeinschaft (WG)	flatshare.
Wohnung (Whg)	flat.
Wohnung gesucht	flat wanted.
zentrale Lage	central location.
Zentralheizung (ZH)	central heating.
Zimmer	room.
Zimmer mit Frühstück	bed and breakfast.
Zu vermieten	to let.

HEALTH AND SOCIAL SECURITY

Social security

Your contributions to social security, together with your employer's share, are deducted at source. They cover pensions, health and unemployment.

Health insurance

You must register with a Krankenkasse (health insurance company which is part of the social security system). Depending on your occupation, you may have a choice of several different Krankenkassen (*eg* KKH, DAK or AOK). Their charges and service are very similar. It is advisable to choose one which has a branch near where you live or work.

If in doubt, register with the Allgemeine Ortskrankenkasse (AOK), which is open to all occupations and has branches in virtually every town, so you don't have to change your registration when you are moving house or changing jobs.

Seeing a doctor

Your Krankenkasse will give you a Krankenscheinheft, a 'cheque-book' with vouchers for medical and dental treatment. For each visit to a doctor or dentist, you fill in one of the vouchers, a Krankenschein, and hand it to the receptionist at the surgery.

Pensions

Contributions are calculated at 17 per cent of gross salary. The employer pays half of this contribution.

Under EU regulations, if you work in two or more EU countries, you can combine the state pension contributions paid in each state to qualify for a state pension. For details, get in touch with the Bundesversicherungsanstalt für Angestellte (the national insurance organisation for employees). Address: Ruhrstr. 2, Berlin-Wilmersdorf, D-10704 Berlin, Germany.

The European Commission has published a guide *Social Security for Migrant Workers*, which is available from The Benefits Directorate, Overseas Branch, Newcastle Upon Tyne, NE98 1YZ, UK. Tel (0191) 213 5000.

PAYING TAXES

Income tax

Income tax (Lohnsteuer or Einkommensteuer) is deducted at source.

When starting employment, you must apply for a Lohnsteuerkarte (income tax card), usually at the Einwohnermeldeamt.

The tax scale increases in proportion to your income. It lies between 22 per cent and 53 per cent of the income. For information, contact the nearest Finanzamt (inland revenue office).

Church tax

If you belong to a church, either catholic or protestant, this will be entered in your Lohnsteuerkarte, and you have to pay church tax, which is calculated at nine per cent of your income tax. If you don't belong to a church, tell the Finanzamt, and you won't have to pay.

BANKING

Wages are normally paid monthly at the end of the month, into a bank account. Open your account as soon as possible. You may want to have two bank accounts, a Sparbuch (savings account) and a Gehaltskonto (current account). The bank will ask to see your passport and will require an initial deposit.

There are many banks in every German town — Volksbank, Bank für Gemeinwirtschaft, Sparkasse, Dresdner Bank etc — and you should select one with many branches in the area, because in Germany you can bank with any of the branches which are linked together in one region.

Alternatively, if you are expecting to transfer money to and from your home country frequently, it is advisable to go to the Deutsche Bank, which has most foreign dealings, but it doesn't have many branches in rural areas.

MAKING FRIENDS

The first months in a foreign country can be a period of loneliness and isolation. There are several things you can do to make friends in Germany.

While still at home

- If you plan to move to Germany not immediately, but after a year or more, find yourself a pen-friend in Germany. Pen pal agencies can help for a fee.

- Ask your national hobby organisation (*eg* the British Sub-Aqua

Club) for the address of their German equivalent. Contact the German organisation and ask for branches and clubs in the area to which you are going.

● Ask your national professional organisation about German equivalents, and join the German organisation. You can then get in touch with your professional peer group on arrival.

● If you live in or near London, join the Anglo German Club, which is a social club for British and German people between the age of 20 and 40, who exchange interests and ideas in both languages — everything from music, cinema and theatre to dancing and fine art. Members who can contribute their personality and ideas are welcome. Anabel Meikle, Anglo German Club, PO Box 427, London W8 5QU, UK.

On arrival

● Enrol for a language class.

● Advertise in the classified section of your local paper that you are looking for friends. This is quite customary if someone moves to a new town. But ask a German friend or contact for advice on how to phrase it, to avoid giving a wrong impression.

● Join a hobby group, if possible for a hobby in which you already have the skills, so the language will not present a big problem.

● Enrol for a course at the Volkshochschule (adult education centre).

● Get in touch with your professional peer group.

● Go out to a Kneipe (pub).

● Ask your colleagues to introduce you to other people.

Being a foreigner

Regrettably, foreigners will inevitably encounter some prejudice and discrimination. Germany has allowed thousands of refugees into the country, and has, in addition, been swamped by job seekers from Eastern Europe.

With rising unemployment, many Germans feel that foreigners are taking away their jobs; some Germans get openly hostile and aggressive. While fascist, racist and nationalist Germans are a small minority, they are an active group who make their presence felt, and they can make life uncomfortable for foreigners.

They are often concentrated in certain villages or areas of the city and, if you feel harassed, it can help to move on to another village or town quarter where you will be left in peace.

Nationals from western, central and northern European countries, from North America, Australia and New Zealand are less likely to encounter prejudice and harassment than those from southern and eastern European, Asian and African countries.

Most Germans, however, are internationally minded and keen to seek your friendship. They are interested in different views. Even at a first encounter, you may become involved in a lively discussion about politics or the environment.

If you want to understand the German mentality, read the paperback *Xenophobe's Guide to the Germans*, by Stefan Zeidenitz and Ben Barkow. It covers everything from 'How They See Others' to 'How They See Themselves'. It explains the German principle of Ordnung (order), the German's fears, obsessions, likes and dislikes, the importance of being green, class structure, manners, leisure and pleasure, sense of humour, eating and drinking, health and hygiene.

LEARNING THE LANGUAGE

High German is the official language, written everywhere. Especially in rural areas, local dialects are spoken, which can be difficult to understand for a foreigner who has only learnt high German. In the North, 'st' is pronounced 'st', but in the south they pronounce it 'sht'. The syllable 'ig' at the end of an adjective is pronounced 'ikh' in the north and 'eegh' in the south. There are also grammatical differences.

Most secondary school students study English as a foreign language. English is also the most common foreign language for business and the most widely understood foreign language, followed by French and Russian (in the east).

If possible, learn at least basic German before you start looking for a job. You can study the language in your home country in evening classes.

One organiser with six centres in the UK (Edinburgh, Manchester, Leeds, Birmingham and two in London) is Berlitz, 9-13 Grosvenor

Street, London W1A 3BZ, UK. Tel (0171) 915 0909; fax (0171) 915 022.

Some colleges offer specialised language courses, *eg* 'German for Tourism' or 'German for Business', which is great if they cover your area of work. If you don't have access to a language college, check out your adult education centre's brochure.

Cassette courses for self study allow flexible use of your time. A major supplier is: Linguaphone Language Training, St Giles House, 50 Poland Street, London W1V 4AX, UK. Tel (0171) 287 4050; fax (0171) 287 1656.

If money is tight and you cannot afford course fees or to buy a cassette course, you can borrow a course from your local library at a nominal fee.

An even better option is learning German in Germany — if you can afford it. It is often a good idea to enrol for a week or more at a language college in Germany, and utilise your time in the country to enquire about job opportunities.

ADAPTING TO CHANGE

What to take with you
Certain everyday items which we use at home are available abroad only with difficulty, or at a higher price. It's worth knowing and taking your own supply. British people going to Germany may want to take the following:

- Your favourite foods. Marmite and lemon curd, for example, are not known in Germany.

- Stockings. In Germany, stockings are not very common, tights being the preferred hosiery. This seems strange, as most underwear departments of the big stores sell bodies with suspenders attached. You may have to go to expensive specialist shops, or even to sex shops, to find a selection of stockings.

- Painkillers. Aspirin and paracetamol are available in pharmacies, but are much more expensive than in the UK. Imitations have to use different trade names. Aspirin copies can be recognised by the prefix 'ASS', *eg* 'ASS Ratiopharm'. Imitation products are a little cheaper than the originals, but still costly. Anyway, you won't find painkillers in discount shops or at the grocer's.

- Make-up, foundation and face powder. If you are very fair skinned, you won't be able to find cosmetics to match your complexion. On average, Germans have slightly darker skin tones, and tan more easily. If your British friends compliment you on your lovely sun tan, your German friends may make fun about your pale English looks.

- Imitation perfumes. In the UK, perfumes of almost identical fragrance and quality to the originals are being sold under similar sounding names *eg* 'Java' is 'Jazz', 'Obvious' is 'Obsession' and 'Vanquish' is 'Vanderbuilt'. While you can get those imitation for £2 or £3 in the UK, expect to pay the equivalent of £10 for the same products in Germany.

Apart from the mentioned items, you will get almost everything in German shops.

What to do when in difficulty
If you get into trouble, don't hesitate to go to the Polizei (police), who may be bureaucratic, but are also helpful. When in serious difficulty, contact your embassy. Most embassies are based in Bonn.

If you suffer from loneliness, isolation, depression, homesickness and frustration (common experiences of expatriates, especially during the first year), contact your church or the Samariter (Samaritans). Just talking about your feelings and experiences will help, and it may give you the motivation to take positive steps. If you need to talk to someone in your mother tongue who comes from the same cultural background, the most likely meeting place is a university. Put up a card with your request up at the university's notice board.

The address of the French, Irish and British embassies are:

Französische Botschaft, Kapellenweg 1A, D-53179 Bonn, Germany. Tel (0228) 362031.

Irische Botschaft, Godesberger Allee 119, D-53175 Bonn, Germany. Tel (0228) 376937.

Britische Botschaft, Friedrich-Ebert-Allee 77, D-53113 Bonn, Germany. Tel (0338) 234061.

16
Job-hunting in Switzerland

Wages are high in Switzerland. On average, employees earn two to three times as much as in the UK. Living costs are about 50 per cent higher. This leaves a lot of profit!

Working conditions in Switzerland are often described as 'excellent'. But the hours are long, there are few public holidays, and less annual leave than, for example, in Germany.

Karin works as a bilingual secretary in a small town in northern Switzerland. She was told off by her boss for going to the loo at 11am. She was supposed to suppress her urge until the official break at 12.30! This is probably not a representative example, but anyone who dislikes strict discipline and prefers a relaxed relationship with their boss will probably be happier in another country.

The book you need when you have made up your mind to go is *Living and Working in Switzerland — A Survival Handbook* by David Hampshire.

WATCH OUT FOR DIFFERENT SPELLING

Swiss German differs from High German in both vocabulary and spelling. It is important to remember this when you are sending out your CV or application letter. If you use the services of a professional translator, let them know that you want Swiss German instead of High German, or ask for two versions.

Certain everyday words are loaned from French, such as 'Velo' instead of 'Fahrrad' (bicycle) and 'Jupe' instead of 'Rock' (skirt). The main difference in spelling is that the Swiss don't use ß, they use ss instead. This is important in the words 'Strasse' (road, street, watch out for it in addresses!) and 'Pass' (passport).

CROSS-BORDER COMMUTING

If your job is close to the German, Italian or French border, try and find cheaper accommodation in those countries. This practice is common, but may involve a certain amount of red tape, with customs, residence permits etc. If you live within 10 km of the Swiss border, you become officially a Grenzgänger, a commuter across borders. Not only will you pay less rent (probably) you will also have less difficulty in obtaining a work permit.

Alternatively, you can go and do your food shopping once a week outside Switzerland. Many Swiss go to Germany on Saturday, for example. Bear in mind that there is a limit to how much shopping you may take across the border. Customs officials can give you the details.

FINDING A JOB

Switzerland has one of the lowest unemployment rates in Europe. But it is not easy to find a job there. Employers need to obtain a work permit, Arbeitserlaubnis, for every foreigner on their payroll; and this is only granted if it is impossible to fill the vacancy with a Swiss national.

Even if you are the best qualified candidate, employers will have to reject you.

Case study

Chris, a graphic designer, was invited to a first and even a second interview, was told that she was the best candidate and that she had the job. She handed in her notice and prepared to go to Switzerland. Then she received a letter of 'We regret . . .' from the company. 'We have offered you the position in error. We apologize.'

They could not obtain a work permit for her. The fact that she was the only hundred per cent suitable candidate was not sufficient. Work permits are only issued if there are no suitable candidates at all.

Two months later she received a phone call from the same company. The only two qualified Swiss candidates had proved to be failures. Now the company might be able to obtain a work permit . . . This time she declined. 'I did not want to take the risk a second time.'

WHICH PERMIT DO YOU NEED?

Switzerland does not use the term work permit in its traditional meaning. The residence permit is a combination of both a residence and a work permit. The holder may live in a specified canton and work for a specified employer for a specified time.

Permits are issued after arrival in Switzerland, but only to persons holding an *Assurance of a Residence Permit* or a *Visa for the Purpose of Employment.*

Everyone, including au pairs, volunteers and trainees, must have a permit.

There are several types of permit, but only two of them are likely to be of interest to job hunters.

- **Standard One-Year Permit B**
  Permit B is for specific employment and valid for one year only, but may be renewable at the end of the period.

- **Seasonal Permit A**
  This is for seasonal employment in the building, hotel and tourism industry It can be issued for up to nine months, but in most cases only four or five months are granted. Entry and exit dates have to be strictly adhered to, otherwise you get trouble!

How to obtain a permit

A permit B for permanent work is difficult to obtain unless you have a job, and unless you have the permit B you won't get a permanent job.

One possible way of breaking this vicious circle is by taking on seasonal work, *eg* in the tourism industry. Then the employer is responsible for obtaining a permit A (seasonal work permit). Once you are in Switzerland, you may be able to find a permanent job, but don't expect it to be easy.

For more information, contact the Swiss Embassy in your country. The address in the UK is 16-18 Montagu Place, London W1H 2BQ, UK. Tel (0171) 723 0701.

SPEAKING THE LANGUAGES

Remember that Switzerland has four national languages: German, French, Italian and Rhaetoroman. Unless you speak one of them fluently (the one of the area where you want to work) and have the basics of a second, you will find only the most menial jobs.

The Schweizerische Verkehrszentrale (SVZ, Swiss National Tourist Office) publishes an annual guide to language courses in Switzerland — when and where they take place, how long they last, and

how much they cost. You can study the national languages —
German, French and Italian. The leaflet contains the addresses of
schools, colleges, universities and private schools; it also has addresses of private schools and organisers who run English language
courses during the summer holidays — a chance for native English
teachers.

For an up-to-date copy write to: Swiss National Tourist Office,
Swiss Centre, Swiss Court, London W1V 8EE, UK. Tel (0171) 734
1921.

FINDING QUALIFIED WORK

Most Swiss are highly educated and qualified. Having 15 A-levels is
considered normal. They take their Matura (A Level equivalent) at
about the age of 21, which is not surprising considering the number
of subjects they have to study. University and college education, too,
is thorough and long. This means there are almost always candidates
with suitable qualifications for executive jobs, even if the employers
prefer foreigners.

You may want to study the situations vacant section of various
newspapers; but remember that your chances of being accepted are
small. Arguably the best newspaper for job adverts is: *Neue Zürcher
Zeitung*, Falkenstrasse 11, Postfach 215, CH-8021 Zürich, Switzerland.

It is available from newsagents almost everywhere in Switzerland,
and often abroad.

Agencies

There are many employment agencies, but they can do nothing for
foreign job hunters who do not possess a work permit, except possibly in the nursing sector.

A monthly updated list of approximately 300 agency addresses in
Switzerland is available from Headhunters, Avotek Publishers, for
£16. (See p138 for addresses).

COMPUTING

'Swiss, like German, companies, prefer degree or higher degree
qualified staff with at least two years' work experience after university,' explains Brian Harris of OCC Computer Personnel, a UK-
based agency which recruits staff for Germany and Switzerland.
'Because of work permit restrictions, candidates must inevitably be

highly qualified if they want to find work within the difficult Swiss labour market.'

He says that the computing experts recruited by ICC can expect to earn between SFR60,000 and SFR90,000 — more than they would get elsewhere for the same job. The address is OCC Computer Personnel. 108 Welsh Row, Nantwich, Cheshire CW5 5EY, UK. Tel (01270) 627206; fax (01270) 629168.

TEACHING ENGLISH

Demand for native English teachers is limited, and a high standard of qualifications and experience is necessary. Without a BA degree or a TEFL certificate your chances are almost zero. Knowledge of banking and finance is a great plus, as the financial world is the sector in which the Swiss are most likely to need English.

Teachers are recruited for either one year or summer camps. For up-to-date requirements of various language schools in Switzerland, their working conditions and pay, refer to the book *Teaching English Abroad — Talk Your Way Around The World!* by Susan Griffith.

A list of schools offering language tuition in the summer holidays which may have vacancies for English native teachers is available from the Swiss National Tourist Office.

NURSING

There is a shortage of nurses, because many Swiss women still prefer the traditional role of housewife and give up their job when they get married.

Hospitals in Switzerland have always vacancies for qualified nurses. You can apply directly to hospitals or through an agency. The hospital or the agency will help to obtain a work permit. It must be pointed out, however, that because of rising unemployment in Switzerland, job hunting for nurses is not as easy as it used to be. You are still likely to find a job, but your choice of employment will be limited.

As a rule, it is easier for specialist nursing staff to find employment than for general nurses. It also helps if you are willing to work irregular hours and night shifts, and it is worth mentioning this in your application.

Agencies

When contacting an agency, you must send a detailed CV, copies of all professional certificates and references from all your previous employers, as well as a recent photograph. If geographically possible, the agency will ask you to come to a personal interview.

Many agencies actively encourage foreign applicants. Hospi Personal in St Gallen is one of them. Christoph Schaufelberger explains: 'We recruit nursing personnel mainly from western Germany and, in recent months, from eastern Germany as well. However, we find that nurses from the east don't have quite the high standard of qualification as those who trained in the west. They also tend to have a relaxed attitude to work, which is not appreciated by Swiss employers!

'We are keen to recruit more staff from the Czech Republic and from Hungary, because they have excellent training standards. However, it is extremely difficult at the moment to obtain work permits for them.

'Good German is essential for most jobs. Patients need nurses who understand their language, and older patients in particular may feel more at ease if they can speak and hear their local accent.'

Hospi Personal is currently looking for OPS and IPS nurses.

Françoise Vauclair, assistant at the Schweizerische Vermittlungs-stelle für Personal des Gesundheitswesens (SVAP), says: 'Qualified nurses with additional training as anethestists, or in IPS and OPS, are most in demand. There are good opportunities, too, for experienced midwives and physiotherapists, who are willing to stay for approximately eighteen months.'

She thinks that general hospital nurses who are 'modestly qualified' will have more difficulty.

'They are most likely to find employment in rural geriatric hospitals,' she advises.

SVAP helps to recruit nursing personnel particularly from Germany, Austria, the Netherlands and Finland.

Useful addresses
The Swiss Embassy in London suggests that applicants contact the following agencies which specialise in nursing work:

Hospi Personal, Rosenbergstrasse 51, CH-9000 St Gallen, Switzerland. Tel (071) 235033; fax (071) 235080.

Agnes Frick Spitalpersonal, Neustadtgasse 7, CH-8024 Zürich, Switzerland. Tel (01) 262 0680; fax (01) 261 2682.

Permed Leuthold & Partner, Seidengasse 10, CH-8001 Zürich, Switzerland. Tel (01) 211 7822.

Schweiz. Vermittlungsstelle für ausl. Pflegepersonal, Weinbergstrasse 29, CH-8006 Zürich, Switzerland. Tel (01) 252 5222.

Schweiz. Vermittlungsstelle für Personal des Gesundheitswesens (SVAP), Schaffhauserstrasse 21, Postfach 51, CH-8024 Zürich, Switzerland. Tel (01) 363 8404; fax (01) 361 5475.

Schweizer Berufsverband der Krankenschwestern und Krankenpfleger, Choisystrasse 1, Postfach 8124, CH-3001 Bern, Switzerland. Tel (031) 381 6427; fax (031) 381 6970.

Case study

Mik, a trained nurse and midwife from Belgium, applied when she heard that the Swiss embassy actively invited applications from nurses. 'It was really easy to find a job. I found one near Fribourg. There were no problems about a permit in the first year, but after one year the permit had to be renewed.' Her main aim was to improve her French, and she says she has become quite fluent, and has mastered the nursing terminology.

'The level of work is about the same as in Belgium or the UK, but everything is more strict. I also found that people were quite reserved, they don't invite you home easily, for example. It took a long time until they got used to me.'

CASUAL AND TEMPORARY WORK

Casual work is quite another matter. The Swiss don't like ordinary work, particularly repetitive and dirty jobs. Employers pay high wages for this type of work, and are willing and able to obtain work permits for foreigners.

Most permit A casual workers come from Italy, Spain or Portugal. They work in tourism, agriculture or the construction industry.

For seasonal work, contact: Jobs in the Alps, 2 West Eaton Place, London SW1X 8LX.

Tourism

Agriculture is extensive in Switzerland and there are many fruit picking temp jobs. However, many farmers prefer to employ farm volunteers (who receive board, lodging and pocket money) instead of employing fully paid temp workers.

If you want to work in the tourism industry, Switzerland is a paradise. Not only is there a shortage of cleaners, chambermaids, kitchen personnel and even shop assistants, but when the season is over at the lakes, another season begins in the skiing areas. In fact, it is easier to find temp jobs in tourism during the winter months (December - April) than in summer (July - September).

Skiing holiday organisers recruit strong **parallel skiers** with experience in working with children and knowledge of mountain safety, for one to four weeks at Christmas, in February and at Easter.

Skiing camps also need **nursing staff**. If you are a registered nurse and are looking for a short term change — a few weeks only — you can apply. Staff at skiing camp receive full board and accommodation, but payment is low.

Chalet girls are in demand, too; they have to commit themselves for several weeks or months. Catering experience or a cookery certificate is often required, but some organisers provide training in cookery skills.

Hotel and catering work is physically demanding, and unpaid extra hours are often required. However, payment for hotel jobs is better than in most other European countries, and it is also better than in the holiday or skiing camps.

Dishwashers, waiters/waitresses, chambermaids, and **laundry maids** can find jobs if they apply at least three months before the season begins. There are also occasional vacancies for animators, computer animators, life guards, receptionists, assistant kindergarten teachers, elevator operators and night porters with the big hotels.

For hotel work, contact: Swiss Hotel Association, Department of Employment, Montbijoustrasse 130, Postfach 2657, CH-3001 Bern, Switzerland. Tel (031) 46 1881.

If you are looking for tourist office employment, the Swiss National Tourist Office in London suggests the following contact: Tourist Office Malcantone, Alfonso Passera, Director, CH-6987 Caslano, Switzerland. Tel (091) 71 2986.

Running up and down the hills
A good seasonal job is that of a postie; demanding, but well paid.

Case study
Suzanne, who had a three month summer contract, described the work as 'physically and mentally exhausting'. Her three predeces-

sors had all given up within two weeks. (By comparison, Heidi, who had a similar job in Germany, described it as 'relaxing and fun'). A postie in Switzerland has plenty of exercise (running up and down the mountains in some areas), fresh air, a demanding round, and excellent pay. She could live several months on what she had earned that summer.

How to find temp jobs

Overseas Job Express is a bi-weekly newspaper with information about job hunting abroad. Employers can advertise their jobs free of charge. Under the classified headings 'sports', 'tourism' or 'catering', there are often vacancies for temp jobs in Switzerland.

For hotel and tourism jobs, refer to the latest edition of *Summer Jobs Abroad*. This annual guide contains an update of hotel addresses, together with job descriptions for temp staff they plan to recruit this year, working conditions and payment (Make sure you have the latest issue!)

BECOMING A FARM VOLUNTEER

If you are prepared to work hard for little money, and are interested in learning about where the food comes from and how a farm works, you can become a farm volunteer.

Volunteers are actively encouraged by the Swiss government. Many young Swiss people join, but about 15 per cent of the participants are from abroad, especially from Poland and the Czech Republic.

They receive free board and lodging at the farm, plus pocket money. Officially, there are about eight working hours per day and six working days per week, but depending on the type of job, you may find that you have to work longer hours.

Apply at least four weeks before you want to start. However, it is not always possible to get a placement confirmed more than a few months in advance. This can be a drawback for travellers working their way around the world who want to make long term travel arrangements.

Knowledge of German or French is essential; farming experience is not necessary.

For an application form (in either German or French), write to: Landdienst-Zentralstelle, Mühlegasse 13, Postfach 728, CH-8025 Zürich, Switzerland. Tel (01) 261 4488.

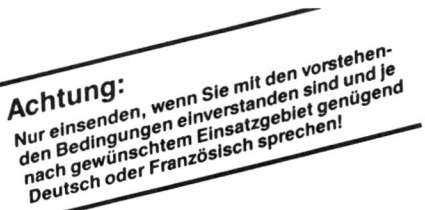

Achtung:
Nur einsenden, wenn Sie mit den vorstehen-
den Bedingungen einverstanden sind und je
nach gewünschtem Einsatzgebiet genügend
Deutsch oder Französisch sprechen!

Anmeldung zum freiwilligen Landdienst
(Bitte in Blockschrift ausfüllen)

Name: _____   Vorname: _____
weiblich/männlich (Nichtzutreffendes streichen)

Geburtsdatum: _____
(Tag, Monat, Jahr)

Staatsangehörigkeit: _____

Genaue Wohnadresse (inkl. Telefonnummer und Name des Landes):

_____

_____

Ausbildung(en): / Berufliche Tätigkeit(en): _____

(weitere Angaben auf der Rückseite dieses Blattes)

Ich möchte den Landdienst vom _____ bis _____ in der
deutschsprachigen Schweiz / französischsprachigen Schweiz leisten.
(Nichtzutreffendes streichen)

Haben Sie schon einmal auf einem Bauernhof gearbeitet? Ja – Nein

Wie lange? _____   Wo? _____

Ich spreche und verstehe   Deutsch   (gut, mittel, schlecht)
                    Französisch   (gut, mittel, schlecht)
                    Englisch   (gut, mittel, schlecht)

(Nichtzutreffendes streichen)

Bemerkungen/Wünsche: _____

_____

(weitere Angaben auf der Rückseite dieses Blattes)

Datum: _____

Unterschrift: _____   Für nicht volljährige Freiwillige
geben das Einverständnis
die Eltern oder der Vormund:

_____   _____

– hier abtrennen –

Fig. 8. Application form for voluntary farm work in Switzerland.

Translation:

Attention: send only if you agree with the conditions and if you have sufficient German or French for the requested area

Registration for voluntary farm work
(Please complete in block capitals)

Name: _____   First name: _____
                                                                   (male/female - delete as appropriate)
Date of birth: _____
(day, month, year)
Nationality: _____

Precise address (incl telephone and country):
_____
_____

Training and experience: _____
_____
(continue on the reverse)

I want to do voluntary farm service from _____ tc _____ in the
German/French speaking part of Switzerland
(delete as appropriate)

Have you worked on a farm before? Yes/no

How long? _____ Where?   _____

I speak and understanc   German   (good, reasonable, poor)
                                     French   (good, reasonable, poor)
                                     English   (good, reasonable, poor)

                                     (delete as appropriate)

Remarks/requests: _____
_____
(continue on the reverse)

Date: _____

Signature: (If under age, signature of parents)

_____   _____

Fig. 8. Translation.

Freiwilliger Landdienst in der Schweiz

Informationen und Anmeldeformular für junge Leute aus Westeuropa
(Aufgrund der Bestimmungen der Arbeitsmarktbehörden können Interessenten aus Osteuropa und Übersee in der Regel nicht berücksichtigt werden)

Der Landdienst bietet jungen Leuten die Möglichkeit, als einzeln eingesetzte Helferinnen und Helfer während maximal zwei Monaten konkreten Einblick in den Alltag einer Schweizer Bauernfamilie zu erhalten. Neben freier Unterkunft und Verpflegung erhalten die Teilnehmer von der Bauernfamilie eine Barentschädigung, Taggeld genannt. Die Vermittlung und die Besorgung der Formalitäten zur Regelung des Arbeitsaufenthaltes sind kostenlos, wenn die Anmeldung nicht zurückgezogen und die Stelle angetreten wird.

Landdienst ist gelegentlich harte, in der Regel abwechslungsreiche Arbeit, die je nach Jahreszeit und Art des Betriebes ganz verschieden sein kann. Neben der Möglichkeit, einen neuen Kulturraum kennenzulernen, können bei Arbeiten auf dem Feld, in Haus, Garten und Stall neue manuelle Fähigkeiten entdeckt und bereits vorhandene Sprachkenntnisse verbessert werden. Einsatzwünsche wie Kinderbetreuung oder Arbeit mit Tieren werden nach Möglichkeit berücksichtigt.

Fachliche Vorkenntnisse sind keine Bedingung für einen Einsatz. Neben ausreichenden Sprachkenntnissen zur Verständigung werden jedoch eine durchschnittliche körperliche Leistungsfähigkeit und Leistungsbereitschaft vorausgesetzt (Der Bauer und die Bäuerin sind angehalten, auf die individuelle Belastbarkeit der Landdiensthilfen Rücksicht zu nehmen und sie zweckmässig anzulernen). In der flächenmässig kleineren französischsprachigen Schweiz können ausländische Teilnehmer wegen dem beschränkten Platzangebot nur ausserhalb der Schweizer Schulferienzeiten berücksichtigt werden. Einsätze in der italienischsprachigen Schweiz sind im Einzelfall möglich. Stellen im Dienstleistungssektor sowie in Betrieben der Industrie und des Gewerbes werden nicht vermittelt.

Die umstehenden Bedingungen sind vor der Anmeldung genau durchzulesen.

Landdienst – eine gute Idee

Die von den Schweizer Kantonen, dem Bund und den bäuerlichen Verbänden unterstützte Schweizerische Landdienst-Vereinigung vermittelt jährlich mehreren tausend inländischen Jugendlichen und zusätzlich, im Sinne der Öffnung und der internationalen Verständigung, etwa 600 jungen Ausländern einen Job auf dem Bauernhof. Wichtige Anliegen sind landesintern der Brückenschlag zwischen Stadt und Land, zwischen den verschiedenen Sprachregionen, Konsumenten und Produzenten. Die Einsatzplätze werden von den kantonalen Vermittlungsstellen beaufsichtigt, die auch die Beratung und Vermittlung der Schweizer Teilnehmer besorgen. Die Vereinigung ist Kontaktmitglied der Schweizerischen Arbeitsgemeinschaft der Jugendverbände (SAJV) sowie des Schweizerischen Dachverbandes der Jugendaustauschorganisationen (Intermundo).

Form. L12/93

Fig. 8. Continued.

Einsatzdauer: mindestens drei Wochen, längstens zwei Monate

Alter: mindestens 17jährig und in der Regel höchstens 30jährig

Einsatzmöglichkeiten: deutschsprachige Schweiz:
von Anfang März bis Ende Oktober

französischsprachige Schweiz:
von Mitte April bis Ende Juni und
von Mitte August bis Ende September

Anmeldung: Mit nebenstehendem Anmeldeformular spätestens 4 Wochen vor dem gewünschten Stellenantritt an die Zentralstelle. **Wenn die Anmeldung nicht via eine anerkannte Anmeldestelle im Ausland erfolgt, muss ein gedeckter Check im Betrag von Schweizer Franken (SFr.) 80.– und zugunsten der Landdienst-Zentralstelle beigelegt werden.** Wird die Anmeldung zurückgezogen oder die Stelle nicht angetreten, so wird der Check zur Deckung der administrativen Kosten eingelöst, andernfalls vernichtet.

Abmeldung: Bereits angemeldete Personen, die am Landdienst nicht teilnehmen können, sind für eine sofortige Abmeldung verantwortlich.

Platzzuteilung: Die Vermittlungsanzeige wird schriftlich zugestellt. Angemeldete Personen, die 10 Tage vor dem gewünschten Einsatztermin noch keine Mitteilung erhalten haben, sollten sich bei der Zentralstelle melden.

Taggeld (Barentschädigung): Neben Unterkunft und Verpflegung, Versicherungsprämien, Aufenthaltsgebühr und Vermittlungsbeitrag bezahlen der Bauer/die Bäuerin den Helfern je Arbeitstag, zufriedenstellende Arbeitsleistungen vorausgesetzt, mindestens SFr. 20.– bar.

Arbeits- und Freizeit: Sonn- und Feiertage sind arbeitsfrei. Die Helferinnen und Helfer können sich an diesen Tagen bei der Gastfamilie verpflegen. **Die wöchentliche Arbeitszeit beträgt maximal 48 Stunden.**

Fahrten: Die Kosten für die Hin- und Rückreise gehen ohne anderweitige Abmachungen vollumfänglich zu Lasten der Teilnehmerinnen und Teilnehmer.

Versicherungen: Die Versicherungen der Bauernfamilie und die Landdienst-Zusatzversicherung bieten ausreichend Schutz bei Unfall oder Krankheit. **Bei Nichtbestehen einer Krankenversicherung für Auslandaufenthalte und einer Haftpflichtversicherung wird ein Abschluss im Heimatland empfohlen.**

Beratung und Betreuung: Die Zentralstelle ist gerne bereit, weitere Auskünfte zu geben. Während dem Einsatz festgestellte Unzulänglichkeiten oder Beanstandungen sind unbedingt mitzuteilen. Umplazierungen sind in der Regel möglich.

Vermittlungsstelle: Landdienst-Zentralstelle
Postfach 728, CH-8025 Zürich
Telefon 01 / 261 44 88
Telefax 01 / 261 44 32

Fig. 8. Continued.

125

SPENDING A YEAR AS AN AU PAIR

As in most countries, au pairs are in demand. They take care of the children, sometimes teach them English and do some housework in return for board, lodging and pocket money. Basic German is usually required, but there is spare time to attend language courses.

The Swiss prefer au pairs from either Europe (especially from the Scandinavian countries), from the United States of America or from Canada.

Au pair positions can be found through agencies in Switzerland or abroad. Agencies usually charge a fee for registration and/or placement. Take care, if you take up an au pair position without the assistance of an agency, that you receive a contract similar to the internationally accepted standard agreement for au pairs. In Switzerland it is important to make sure that your employer sorts out your residence permit.

To ensure that you really are an au pair, and not unofficially employed as a private teacher or housekeeper, authorities may require proof that you have enrolled with a language school.

If you are lucky, your employer may, in addition to pocket money, contribute towards your travel and language course expenses.

Useful addresses

The Swiss Embassy in London suggests the following agencies which recruit candidates from abroad for au pair work in the German speaking area:

Verein der Freundinnen junger Mädchen, Ahornweg 106, CH-3095 Spiegel/Bern, Switzerland. Tel (031) 971 26 56.

Verein der Freundinnen junger Mädchen, Steinengraben 69, CH-3095 Basel, Switzerland. Tel (061) 271 3319.

Pro Filia, Beckenhofstrasse 16, CH-8035 Zürich, Switzerland. Tel (01) 363 5501.

Verein der Freundinnen junger Mädchen, Zähringerstrasse 36, CH-8001 Zürich, Switzerland. Tel (01) 252 3840.

An agency recruiting au pairs from the UK for Switzerland is:

- South Eastern Au Pair Bureau, 37 Rutland Avenue, Thorpe Bay, Essex SS1 2XJ, UK. Tel (01702) 601911.

SUMMARY

- You will only be offered a job if it is impossible to fill the vacancy with a Swiss national.

- Swiss working practices are less relaxed than in many other countries.

- Commuting across the border to your job in Switzerland may be cheaper than living there.

- It is essential that you can speak at least one of the national languages fluently.

- Nurses, particularly those with specialist training, can find good jobs.

- Swiss employers demand high qualifications from foreign applicants.

- Casual work is available in catering, tourism and agriculture.

- Good prospects exist for au pairs.

17
Job-hunting in Austria

Most foreigners working in Austria come from the area of the former Yugoslavia, followed by Turkey, Germany and Poland. A great number come from Hungary, Rumania, the former Czechoslovakia, and the Philippines.

In 1993 there were 1,298 UK nationals working in Austria.

The strongest industries in Austria are engineering, light manufacturing, steel and iron, agriculture, tourism, food, chemicals, textiles and paper.

Your chances are much better if you write and speak German. Austrian German is very similar to High German; spelling and grammar are the same. Only a few words differ: 'Cream' is 'Sahne' in High German and 'Schlagobers' in Austrian German — important for waiters.

LEARNING THE LANGUAGE

The Austrian Embassy in London emphasises that a profound knowledge of German is essential for any type of employment, with the exception of au pair jobs.

Prospective applicants may consider going on a holiday to Austria first, combining a language course with enquiries about job prospects.

Vienna International University Courses runs courses at six different levels of the German language, which often include literature, music, art and linguistics and are open to students of 16 years and older. They conclude with an optional examination, and there are 20 students per class. Tuition for four weeks costs around AS3,550. Additional costs are a registration fee (AS200), textbooks (AS400) and accommodation (AS6,700).

For information write to: Sekretariat der Wiener Internationalen Hochschulkurse, Universität, A-1010 Wien, Austria. Tel (01) 421254 or 424737; fax (01) 421254/10.

The Austro-American Society, in cooperation with the Goethe Institute, also offers four week sessions in German for foreigners at different levels The fee is at present AS3,800 for one session, AS7,500 for two. Write to: Austro-American Society, Stallburggasse 2, A-1010 Wien, Austria. Tel (01) 5123982 or 5124784; fax (01) 513 9123.

Very advanced students, professionals, executives, translators and interpreters can book private instruction at the Sprachinstitut der Industrie (SPIDI). A five day course costs AS19,500, each additional day AS3,000. Students may choose any dates they want, including weekends. Write to: Sprachinstitut der Industrie, Lothringergasse 12, A-1031 Wien, Austria. Tel (01) 7152506/2623; fax (01) 711 352917.

Up-to-date information about language classes can be obtained from: Austrian Institute, 28 Rutland Gate, London SW7, UK. Tel (0171) 584 8653.

GETTING A RESIDENCE PERMIT

Work and residence permits are not required for nationals of EU and EEA countries.

All other nationalities need work and residence permits for all types of work, including au pair placements.

To obtain a residence permit, apply to the Austrian embassy in your country of residence, who will send you an application form. However, it is the authorities in Austria, not the embassies abroad, who make the decision.

Work permits can only be applied for by your future employer, so you have to find a job first.

HOW TO FIND PERMANENT WORK

Similar to the German Zentralstelle für Arbeitsvermittlung, there is an Austrian state employment service, the Arbeitsamt.

Contact the Arbeitsamt in the Bundesland where you wish to work. All applicants must be made in writing, in German language, and contain the following details: name and address, date of birth, education, profession, type of present employment, knowledge of foreign languages, length of intended stay and type of job required.

Landesarbeitsamt für das Burgenland, Permayerstr. 10, A-7001 Eisenstadt, Austria.

Landesarbeitsamt für Kärnten, Kumpfgasse 25, A-910 Klagenfurt, Austria.

Landesarbeitsamt für Niederösterreich, Hohenstauffengasse 2, A-1013 Wien, Austria.

Landesarbeitsamt für Salzburg, Auerspergstr. 67a, A-5021 Salzburg, Austria.

Landesarbeitsamt für Tirol, Schöpfstr. 5, A-8010 Innsbruck, Austria.

Landesarbeitsamt für Steiermark, Babenbergerstr. 33, A-8021 Graz, Austria.

Landesarbeitsamt für Vorarlberg, Rheinstr. 32, A-6801 Bregenz, Austria.

Landesarbeitsamt für Wien, Weihburggasse 30, A-1011 Wien, Austria.

VACATION AND TEMP WORK

For casual employment, consult the latest copy of *Summer Jobs Abroad* or of the newspaper *Overseas Job Express*.

Most vacancies are in the **hotel and catering** sector: lots of kitchen assistants, chambermaids, washers-up, waiters/waitresses and bar staff are needed, as well as some souvenir shop assistants, drivers, lifeguards and receptionists.

During the winter months, chances in the **skiing** areas are good. In summer, both the mountains and the lakes become hunting grounds for job hunters. Occasionally, English speaking skiing instructors, windsurf instructors and animators are needed.

Vacancies in **agriculture** and **farming** are limited; you may find a job during the grape harvesting season.

Students who seek short-term or holiday employment, especially **voluntary work**, can contact the following organisations.

Central Bureau for Educational Visits and Exchanges, Seymour Mews House, Seymour Mews, London W1H 9PE, UK.

Austrian Committee for the International Exchange of Students, Türkenstr. 4, A-1090 Wien, Austria.

AU PAIRING

To find au pair placements, refer to *Overseas Job Express*, or contact the following addresses:

Sandra Clarke, South Eastern Au Pair Bureau, 39 Rutland Avenue, Thorpe Bay, Essex SS1 2XJ, UK. Tel (01702) 601911.

Auslands-Sozialdienst, Johannesgasse 16, A-1010 Wien, Austria.

TEACHING

Teachers have civil servant status in the Austrian state school system and therefore have to be Austrian citizens. A limited programme for the exchange of teachers is being run by the Federal Ministry for Education, Arts and Sports in Wien (Vienna). Information about this programme is available from the Central Bureau for Educational Visits and Exchanges (address on page 130).

There are a number of schools in Vienna with English as the main working language. The Austrian Embassy in London suggests that teachers who are English native speakers can apply there for employment:

American International School, Salmannsdorferstr. 45-47, A-1190 Wien, Austria.

Vienna International School, Geymüllergasse 1, A-1190 Wien, Austria.

English Teaching School, Grinzingerstr. 95, A-1190 Wien, Austria.

LIVING IN AUSTRIA

All employees (except au pairs) must participate in the health and social security scheme, which also includes a pension scheme and covers most medical expenses, including hospital treatment.

Social security contributions and income tax are deducted from gross wages by your employer.

USEFUL ADDRESSES

● Österreichisches Statistisches Zentralamt, Hintere Zollamtstr. 2b, A-1033 Wien, Austria. Tel (01) 711280.

British Trade Council in Austria, Mollwald-Platz 1/12, A-1040 Wien, Austria.

Austrian Trade Commission, 1 Hyde Park Gate, London SW7 5ER, UK. Tel (0171) 854 4411; fax (0171) 584 2565.

Bundeskammer der gewerblichen Wirtschaft, Stubenring 8-10, A-1010 Wien, Austria. Tel (01) 514500; fax (01) 513 7787.

Verkehrsamt der Bundespolizeidirektion Wien, Türkenstr. 22a, A-1090 Wien, Austria.
(about vehicle registration and driving licence validation)

Bundesministerium für Arbeit und Soziales (Federal Ministry for Labour and Social Affairs), Stubenring 1, A-1011 Wien, Austria.

SUMMARY

● To find employment in Austria, you must speak German.

● Register with the Arbeitsamt of the region where you want to live.

Further Reading

NEWSPAPERS AND MAGAZINES

Overseas Jobs Express
Bi-weekly newspaper which not only contains lots of situations vacant advertisements (foreign employers can advertise their vacancies free of charge), but is crammed with features and advice for job hunters, as well as personal experience reports. *Overseas Job Express*, PO Box 22, Brighton BN1 5HX, UK. Tel (01273) 440220.

Escape — The Career Change Magazine
Bi-monthly magazine with features and advice for anyone who wants to take their career in a different direction, including going abroad. Weavers Press Publishing, Paul King, 113 Abbot Ann Down, Andover, Hampshire SP11 7BX.

Jobs International
Monthly magazine with features and news articles about job-hunting abroad. Annual subscription £30. Cromwell Court, New Road, St Ives, Cambridgeshire PE17 4BG.

Pro-Job
German language monthly magazine with features, news, addresses and advice for job-hunting and careers. DM4.50 per issue. Hans-Böckler-Allee 7, Postfach 5440, D-30173, Hannover, Germany. Tel (0511) 85500; fax (0511) 8550402.

BOOKS

Guide to Working Abroad
Godfrey Golzen, published by Kogan Page with *The Daily Telegraph*. Paperback, 314 pages with invaluable advice — mostly on financial matters — for expatriates. Slanted at people in higher income brackets who plan on staying long term or permanently

abroad. Probably of less interest to young travellers who work their way across the world. There is a chapter on Germany and one on Switzerland, but Austria is not covered.

Teaching English Abroad — Talk Your Way Around the World
Susan Griffith, published by Vacation Work, 9 Park End Street, Oxford, UK. Paperback, 320 pages. This useful guide for language teachers is in two individual parts. The first gives plenty of information about qualifications, rewards, risks and job hunting; the second is a country-by-country guide of potential employers with full addresses, stating job descriptions, working conditions and payment. There is a long chapter on Germany and a short one on Switzerland, but nothing on Austria.

Summer Jobs Abroad
David Woodworth and Giles Smart (eds), published by Vacation Work, 9 Park End Street, Oxford, UK. This annual guide gives some information on how to apply for a job, visas, residence and work permits, au pair work etc. But the best part of the book is the country-by-country guide of available summer (and winter) jobs, complete with addresses, required language skills and experience, payment, accommodation, expected duration of stay etc. Most vacancies listed are in the hotel and catering sector, *eg* chambermaids, waiters/waitresses, and kitchen assistants. If you plan on working your way around Europe and want to stay several weeks or months in Germany and Switzerland (Austria is not mentioned), this is the book for you. Make sure you have the latest copy — the information is updated every year.

Xenophobe's Guide to The Germans
Stefan Zeidenitz and Ben Barkow, published by Ravette Books, Egmont House, 8 Clifford Street, London W1X 1RB. Paperback, 64 pages. At £2.50 this book is cheap, compact and lightweight enough for any rucksack or hand luggage, and it provides entertaining reading for the journey! The contents are hilarious as well as informative — you will truly understand the German way of living and thinking, as well as have a really good laugh.

Travellers Survival Kit Europe
David Woodworth, published by Vacation Work, 9 Park End Street, Oxford, UK. Paperback, 288 pages. Especially useful for the traveller across many European countries. Lots of advice on public transport,

foreign currency, youth and student travel, communications, plus accommodation etc. It contains a country-by-country guide with information and addresses which includes Germany, Austria and Switzerland.

European Information Pocket Book
Published by NTC Publications Ltd, PO Box 69, Henley-on-Thames, Oxfordshire RG9 1GB, UK. Paperback, 224 pages. An incredible wealth of information for such a compact book. It contains, for example, not only all the embassies and chambers of commerce *of* all European countries *in* all European countries, but the addresses of statistical offices, marketing and advertising associations, market research associations, television and radio organisations, publishing organisations, exhibition organisers, advertising data sources, maps, airlines, airports, train and ferry information, telephone codes and emergency numbers. An updated issue is published annually.

DIRECTORIES

Headhunters Guides
Published by Avotek Publishers, Woerdsestraat 7, NL-6684 DL Ressen, Netherlands. Annually updated directories for Germany (west), Germany (north and east), Germany (south), engineers (Europe), Switzerland. Contain the addresses of most recruitment agencies in the relevant geographical area.

BROCHURES

Working in Germany and *Working Abroad*
Both available free from job centres in the UK, or from The Employment Service, Overseas Placing Unit, Rockingham House, 123 West Street, Sheffield, S1 4ER, UK.

Information on Travel in Germany
26 pages packed with advice and addresses on almost anything a traveller might want to know, including what vaccinations are needed for your pet, the opening hours of hairdressing establishments, phone cards, speed limits, Sunday return train tickets, cycling tours . . .
   Available free (but A5 sae or contribution towards postage is appreciated) from the German National Tourist Office, Nightingale House, 65 Curzon Street, London W1 7PE, UK.

Glossary

Abitur. Higher education examination and school leaving certificate, similar to A-levels but covers more subjects and is therefore taken by students at a slightly older age (at about twenty).

Abteilungsleiter/Abteilungsleiterin. Male/female head of department.

Arbeitgeber. Employer(s).

Arbeitnehmer. Employee(s).

Arbeitsamt. A branch of, or a short word for, the Zentralstelle für Arbeitsvermittlung.

Arbeitserlaubnis. Work permit (not necessary for EU nationals).

Arbeitsvermittlungsagenturen. Recruitment agencies (they must be licensed by the state).

Aufenthaltserlaubnis. Residence permit.

Ausbildung. Training or apprenticeship, lasts around three years. Combines practical work and college studies, strictly regulated and examined by chambers of commerce.

Betriesbrat/Betriebsrätin. Shop steward.

Bewerber/Bewerberin. Male/female applicant.

Bewerbung. Application.

Diplom. University degree, approximately equivalent to UK masters degree.

Einwohnermeldeamt. The authority where you have to register when taking up residence in Germany.

Formular. form.

Freiwilliges Soziales Jahr. One year of voluntary work for young people, usually in hospitals.

Landdienst. Voluntary farm work in Switzerland.

Lebenslauf. CV.

Matura. Higher secondary education examination in Switzerland, the equivalent of the German Abitur.

Mittlere Reife. Secondary school education examination and school leaving certificate, taken at about sixteen, would rank approximately between UK O- and A-levels,

Sachbearbeiter/ Sachbearbeiterin. Executive, manager (lower management).

Sozialversicherung. Social security.

Stellenangebote. Situations vacant advertisements.

Stellengesuche. Situations wanted advertisements.

Tarifvertrag. Collective agreement about wages and working conditions in a particular industry sector, negotiated by the trade unions and the employers.

Urlaubsanspruch. Annual leave entitlement.

Zeitarbeit. Temporary work.

Zentralstelle für Arbeitsvermittlung. The German state employment service.

Useful Addresses

STATE EMPLOYMENT ORGANISATIONS

The Employment Service, Overseas Placing Unit, Rockingham
House, 123 West Street, Sheffield, S1 4ER, UK. Tel (0114)
2596051; fax (0114) 2596040.

Zentralstelle für Arbeitsvermittlung, Feuerbachstr. 42-46, D-60325
Frankfurt, Germany. Tel (069) 71110; fax (069) 7111-540.

RECRUITMENT AGENCIES

European Affairs, 10 Buckley Road, St Neots, Cambridgeshire,
PE19 2TR, UK.

Hospi-Personal, Rosenbergstr. 51, CH-9000 St. Gallen, Switzerland.
Tel (071) 235033; fax (071) 235080.

Jobs in the Alps, 2 West Eaton Place, London SW1X 8LX, UK. Tel
(0171) 235 8205.

Landdienst-Zentrale, Mühlegasse 13, Postfach 728, CH-8025 Zürich,
Switzerland. Tel (01) 261 4488.

OCC Computer Personnel, 108 Welsh Row, Nantwich, Cheshire,
CW5 5EY, UK. Tel (01270) 627206; fax (01270) 629168.

Pro Filia, Beckenhofstr. 16, CH-8035 Zürich, Switzerland. Tel (01)
363 5501.

Schweizerische Vermittlungs- und Beratungsstelle für Personal des
Gesundheitswesens AG, Schaffhauserstr. 21, Postfach 51, CH-
7042 Zürich, Switzerland. Tel (01) 363 8404; fax (01) 361 5474.

Solihull Au Pair & Nanny Agency, 1565 Stratford Road, Hall Green,
Birmingham B28 9JA, UK. Tel (0121) 733 644; fax (0121) 733
6555.

South Eastern Au Pair Bureau, 39 Rutland Avenue, Thorpe Bay,
Essex, SS1 2XJ, UK. Tel (01702) 601911.

Verein der Freundinnen junger Mädchen, Zähringerstr. 36, CH-8001
Zürich, Switzerland. Tel (01) 252 3840.

WORK AND TRAINING RELATED INSTITUTIONS

The Comparability Coordinator/Training, Enterprise and Education Directorate, Department of Employment, Moorfoot, Sheffield, S1 4PQ, UK. Tel (0114) 2753275; fax (0114) 2758316/2594724.

National Council for Vocational Qualifications, 222 Euston Road, London NW1 2BZ, UK. Tel (0171) 3879898; fax (0171) 3870978.

TRADE COUNCILS AND CHAMBERS OF COMMERCE

The British Council, Hahnenstr. 6, D-50667 Köln, Germany. Tel (0221) 2064433; fax (0221) 2064455.

The British Council, Lumumbastr. 11-13, D-04105 Leipzig, Germany. Tel (0341) 564 7153; fax (0341) 564 7152.

The British Council, Hardenbergstr. 20, D-10623 Berlin, Germany. Tel (030) 311 0990; fax (030) 311 09920.

The British Chamber of Commerce in Germany Foundation, Heumarkt 14, D-50667 Köln, Germany. Tel (0221) 234284/5.

Chambre Franco-Allemande de Commerce et d'Industrie, 18 rue Balard, F-75015 Paris, France. Tel (01) 4575 6256; fax (01) 4575 4739.

German Chamber of Industry and Commerce, 16 Buckingham Gate, London SW1E 6LB, UK. Tel (0171) 235 5033.

German Federation of Chambers of Commerce, Deutscher Industrie- und Handelstag, Adenauerallee 148, Postfach 1446, D-5300 Bonn, Germany. Tel (0228) 1041; fax (0228) 104158.

Industrie- und Handelskammer Karlsruhe, Postfach 3440, Lammstr. 13-17, D-76020 Karlsruhe, Germany. Tel (0721) 174-0; fax (071) 174-290.

Nederlands-Duitse Kamer van Koophandel, Postbus 80533, NL-2508 GM The Hague, Netherlands. Tel (70) 361 4251; fax (70) 363 2218.

EMBASSIES IN THE UK

Deutsche Botschaft/German Embassy, 23 Belgrave Square, London SW1X 8PZ, UK. Tel: (0171) 235 5033.

Österreichische Botschaft/Austrian Embassy, 18 Belgrave Mews West, London SW1X 8HU, UK. Tel (0171) 235 3731; fax (0171) 235 8025.

Schweizer Botschaft/Swiss Embassy, 16-18 Montagu Place, London W1H 2BQ, UK. Tel (0171) 7230701.

EMBASSIES IN AUSTRIA

Britische Botschaft/British Embassy, 40 Reisnerstr., A-1030 Wien, Austria. Tel (01) 731575; fax (01) 757824.
Irische Botschaft/Irish Embassy, Hilton Centre, 16th Floor, A-1030 Wien, Austria. Tel (01) 715 4246.

EMBASSIES IN SWITZERLAND

Britische Botschaft/British Embassy, Thunstr. 50, CH-3005 Berne, Switzerland. Tel (031) 445021; fax (031) 440583.
Irische Botschaft/Irish Embassy, 68 Kirchenfeldstr., CH-3000 Berne, Switzerland. Tel (031) 440016.

EMBASSIES IN GERMANY

Britische Botschaft/British Embassy, Friedrich-Ebert-Allee 77, D-53113 Bonn, Germany. Tel (0228) 234061.
Irische Botschaft/Irish Embassy, Godesberger Allee 119, D-53175 Bonn, Germany. Tel (0228) 376937.

LANGUAGE SCHOOLS

Berlitz, 9-13 Grosvenor Street, London W1A 3BZ, UK. Tel (0171) 915 0909; fax (0171) 915 0222.
Linguaphone, St Giles House, 50 Poland Street, London W1V 4AX, UK. Tel (0171) 287 4050; fax (0171) 287 1656.
Swiss Federation of Private Schools, Advisory Office, 16 rue du Mont Blanc, POB 1488, CH-1211 Geneva 1, Switzerland. Tel (022) 738 8812; fax (022) 738 88 35.
Austro-American Society, Stallburggasse 2, A-1010 Wien, Austria. Tel (01) 512 3982; fax (01) 513 9123.
Sekretariat der Wiener Internationale Hochschulkurse, Universität, A-1010 Wien, Austria. Tel (01) 421254.
Spidi - Sprachinstitut der Industrie, Lothringerstr. 12, A-1031 Wien, Austria. Tel (01) 715 2506/2623; fax (01) 711 352917.

NATIONAL TOURIST OFFICES

Austrian National Tourist Office, 30 St George's Street, London W1, UK. Tel: (0171) 629 0461.
German National Tourist Office, Nightingale House, 65 Curzon Street, London W1Y 7PE. Tel (0171) 411 3400.

Deutsche Zentrale für Tourismus, Beethovenstr. 69, D-60325 Frankfurt, Germany. Tel (069) 757 20; fax (069) 751903.

Schweizerische Verkehrszentrale/Swiss National Tourist Office, Bellariastr. 38, CH-8027 Zürich, Switzerland. Tel (01) 288 1111; fax (01) 288 1205.

Swiss National Tourist Office, Swiss Centre, Swiss Court, London W1V 8EE, UK. Tel (0171) 734 1921; fax (0171) 437 4577.

TRAVEL AND ACCOMMODATION

Deutsches Jugendherbergswerk, Hauptverband für Jugendwandern und Jugendherbergen e.v., Bismarckstr. 8, Postfach 1455, D-32754 Detmold, Germany. Tel (05231) 7401-0; fax (05231) 7401-49.

DER Travel Service, 18 Conduit Street, London W1 9TD, UK. Tel (0171) 4490577.

German Federal Railway, Suite 118 Hudson's Place, Victoria Station, London SW1 1JL.

OTHER

Aktion Sühnezeichen Friedensdienste e.V., Postfach 154, D-10321 Berlin, Germany. Tel (030) 55 19 03 10; fax (030) 55 19 03 76.

Anglo-German Club, PO Box 427, London W8 5QU, UK.

Arbeitskreis Freiwillige Soziale Dienste, Postfach 10 11 42, D-70010 Stuttgart, Germany. Tel (0711) 2159-0; fax (0711) 2159-288.

Association Internationale des Etudiants en Sciences Economiques et Commerciales (AIESEC), 2nd Floor, 29-31 Cowper Street, London EC2A 4AP, UK. Tel (0171) 336 7939; fax (0171) 336 7971.

Auslands-Sozialdienst, Johannesgasse 16, A-1010 Wien, Austria.

Austrian Committee for the International Exchange of Students (ÖKISTA), Türkenstr. 4, A-1090 Wien, Austria.

The British Institute of International and Comparative Law, Charles Clore House, 17 Russell Square, London WC1B 5DR, UK. Tel (0171) 636 5802.

Bundesministerium für Arbeit und Soziales (Federal Ministry for Labour and Social Affairs), Stubenring 1, A-1011 Wien, Austria. Tel (1) 711 00-1.

Bundesstelle für Außenhandelsinformation (Foreign trade information office), Blaubach 13, Postfach 108007, Köln. Tel (0221) 20571; fax (0221) 2057212.

Bundesversicherungsanstalt für Angestellte, Berlin-Wilmersdorf, Ruhrstr. 2, D-10704 Berlin, Germany.

The Central Bureau, 16 Malone Road, Belfast, BT9 5BN, UK. Tel (0232) 664418.

The Central Bureau, 3 Bruntsfield Crescent, Edinburgh EH10 4HD, UK. Tel (0131) 447 8022.

The Central Bureau, Seymour Mews House, Seymour Mews, London W1H 9PE, UK. Tel (0171) 486 5101.

Christlicher Friedensdienst e.V., Rendelerstr. 9-11, D-60385 Frankfurt. Tel (069) 459072; fax (069) 461213.

Community Action Programme for Education and Training for Technology (Comett), Sanctuary Buildings, Great Smith Street, London SW1P 3BT, UK. Tel (0171) 925 5254; fax (0171) 935 5379.

Deutsche Forschungsgemeinschaft, Referat III 0 6, Kennedyallee 40, Postfach 20 50 04, D-53175 Bonn, Germany. Tel (0228) 8851; fax (0228) 885 2221.

Deutsche Presse-Agentur GmbH (dpa), Mittelweg 38, Hamburg 13. Tel (040) 41131; fax (040) 4113551 (press agency).

Deutscher Akademischer Austauschdienst/German Academic Exchange Service, 17 Bloomsbury Square, London WC1A 2LP, UK. Tel (0171) 4044065; fax (0171) 4302634.

Deutscher Akademischer Austauschdienst/German Academic Exchange Service, Jägerstr. 22-23, D-10117 Berlin, Germany. Tel (030) 231208-0.

Deutscher Gewerkschaftsbund, Hans-Böckler-Str. 39, D-40476 Düsseldorf, Germany. Tel (0211) 430100; fax (0211) 4301471.

German Historical Institute, 17 Bloomsbury Square, London WC1A 2LP, UK. Tel (0171) 404 548.

Government Press and Information Office, Welcherstr 11, Bonn 1. Tel (0228) 2080.

King Edward VII British-German Foundation, 23 Falcondale Road, Westbury on Trym, Bristol BS9 3JS, UK. Tel (0117) 9623613.

Südkurier, Anzeigenbearbeitung, Max-Stromeyer-Str. 178, D-78467 Konstanz, Germany. Tel (07531) 999-0; fax (07531) 999-485.

Swiss Hotel Association, Department of Employment, Monbijoustr. 130, Postfach 2657, CH-3001 Bern, Switzerland. Tel (031) 46 1881.

Tourist Office Malcantone, CH-6987 Casiano, Switzerland. Tel (091) 71 2986.

Index